HISTORY and HAPPENINGS
in the Cariboo-Chilcotin

Pioneer Memories

Irene Stangoe

Heritage House
VANCOUVER • VICTORIA • CALGARY

Heritage House Publishing Company Ltd.
#108 – 17665 66A Avenue
Surrey, BC V3S 2A7
www.heritagehouse.ca

Library and Archives Canada Cataloguing in Publication
Stangoe, Irene, 1918-
    History and happenings in the Cariboo-Chilcotin

Includes index.
    ISBN 13: 978-1-895811-99-5
    ISBN 10: 1-895811-99-6

1. Frontier and pioneer life—British Columbia—Cariboo Region. 2. Frontier and pioneer life—British Columbia—Chilcotin River Region. 3. Pioneers—British Columbia—Cariboo Region—Biography. 4. Pioneers—British Columbia—Chilcotin River Region—Biography. 5. Cariboo Region (B.C.)—Biography. 6. Chilcotin River Region (B.C.)—Biography. 7.Cariboo Region (B.C.)—History. 8. Chilcotin River Region (B.C.)—History. I. Title.

FC3845.C3Z48 2000   971.1'7503'0922   C00-910115-2
F1089.C3S73 2000

Cover design by Darlene Nickull.
Layout by Elizabeth Calver.
Edited by Audrey McClellan.
Front cover photo by Chris Schmid, back cover photo by Irene Stangoe.

Printed in Canada

Heritage House acknowledges the financial support for its publishing program from the Government of Canada through the Book Publishing Industry Development Program (BPIDP), Canada Council for the Arts, and the British Columbia Arts Council.

The Canada Council | Le Conseil des Arts
for the Arts | du Canada

BRITISH COLUMBIA
ARTS COUNCIL
Supported by the Province of British Columbia

Dedication

In memory of my dear friend Carol Shaw, who shared the ups and downs of the Stangoe family for over 60 years. She died November 1, 1997, before she could finish her book on the history of the 100 Mile House.

Acknowledgements

In writing my third book on the Cariboo-Chilcotin, I have had the help of many people. I would like to list all the names, but I'm afraid I will miss someone in the process, so all I can say is a big thank-you to all those who told me their stories, trusted me with photos of bygone days, or passed along a bit of historical information. I truly appreciated each and every contribution in my efforts to preserve a bit more of our heritage.

I do, however, wish to mention local archivist/ historian John Roberts, who has always been there when I needed him with another photograph, a map, or a gem of history.

As usual, much of my information comes from the files of the *Williams Lake Tribune*, which have always been made available to me. Without it, this book would have been a lot longer in the making.

Photo credits

Most photos have been credited throughout the book, whether to the B.C. Archives & Records Service, the *Williams Lake Tribune,* or to the individual sources. All others come from Irene Stangoe's own collection.

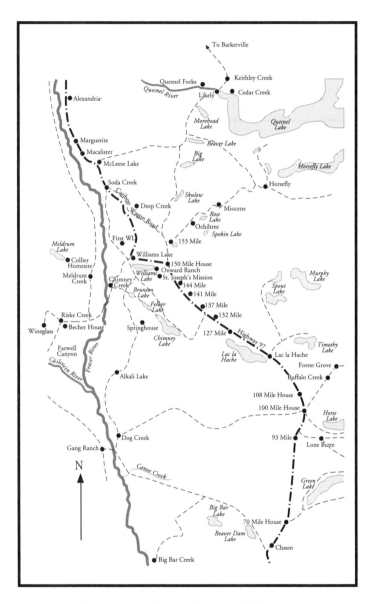

The Central Cariboo-Chilcotin

Contents

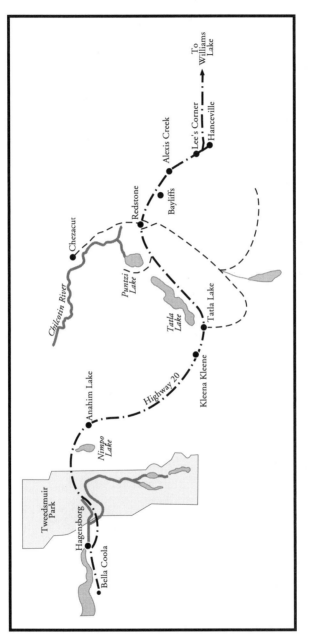

The Central Chilcotin

Dally and the Cariboo Chiefs

One of the finest of B.C.'s early photographers was Frederick Dally, who during the late 1860s produced many priceless images of our province and its people, including my favourite—of a group of Cariboo chiefs taken at New Westminster in 1867.

The native leaders had been invited to the Colony of British Columbia's capital by Governor Frederick Seymour to celebrate Queen Victoria's birthday on May 24.

This was not Seymour's first May 24th celebration, however; he had been staging them since 1864 when he became the second governor of the mainland colony. According to Margaret Ormsby's *British Columbia: A History*, that first celebration was a huge success. "The Indians travelled great distances down the river to take part and for about a week 3,500 of them remained encamped on the outskirts of the town."

> When they finally departed, their canoes were laden with goods which they had purchased in the shops and they gave farewell cheers as they passed Government House. In preparation for their return in a year's time, Seymour ordered from England 100 canes with silver gilt tops engraved with the Crown and 100 small cheap flags.

The Indian chiefs in Dally's photograph are all identified, including Chief William of the Williams Lake Indian Band. Actually this is the second Chief William; he would have been in his late 30s at the time. His father, the first Chief William, died in the terrible smallpox epidemic of 1862, but not before he had made a place for

The photograph of the Cariboo chiefs taken by Frederick Dally at New Westminster in 1867. Standing, left to right, are Tak-o'task, Canoe Creek; William, Williams Lake. Seated: Na-nah, Dog Creek; Quil-quarlse, Alkali Lake; Se-as-kut, Shuswap; Templ-khan, Babine Lake; Silkosalish, Lillooet; Kam-eo-saltze, Soda Creek; Sosastumpl, Bridge Creek. (BCARS C-09263)

himself in the history of the Cariboo by averting war between native people and white men surging into the country searching for gold.

Up to this time Williams Lake had been known as Lake Columneetza, an ancient Athapaskan name, but it was now changed to honour the old Shuswap chief.

Notice all the wonderful details captured on film by Dally, who was an untrained yet extraordinary photographer with a fine eye for composition: the solemn men in native costume posed against a backdrop of gaunt tree stumps and gingerbread homes, a subtle blending of the old with the new.

After emigrating from England to Victoria in 1862 at the height of the gold rush, Dally first set up as a retailer selling everything from engravings to wine goblets and musical instruments. It's not known why he switched to photography, but in 1866 he established his own photography shop.

In his quest for unusual photographs, he first travelled to Vancouver Island with Island governor Arthur Kennedy to record several Indian villages. Then in 1867, and again in 1868, he set out with Governor Seymour for Barkerville, where all the gold-rush madness was concentrated.

"It wasn't easy for a roving photographer travelling to the Cariboo in the 1860s," writes Rosemary Neering in an article on Dally in *Beautiful B.C.* magazine. "Imagine carrying a huge camera, a bulky tripod, dozens of heavy glass plates, a chest of chemicals, distilled water, and darkroom tent to prepare his plates—a far cry from today's small automatic cameras and fast film." Yet he produced some incredible photographs.

Frederick Dally in later years.
(BCARS B-00883)

One of his best known, which is still being reproduced in innumerable magazines and books, is his shot at the Great Bluff in the Fraser Canyon, which shows a covered wagon pulled by a long mule team plodding up the narrow Cariboo Wagon Road through the immense rock defile blasted out by road contractors.

By 1870 the Cariboo gold rush was petering out and Dally decided it was time to leave Victoria. Oddly enough, he launched into a completely new career, enrolling and graduating from the Philadelphia College of Dentistry, then returning to England.

B.C. residents will always be indebted to Frederick Dally for recording our province's early history in his outstanding photographs. We in the Cariboo particularly thank him for his magnificent portrait of our native leaders in bygone days.

This renowned photograph of the Great Bluff in the Fraser Canyon is one of Dally's best-known images.
(BCARS A-00350)

To Go On Is Madness

The great Cariboo gold rush is probably the most fascinating period in British Columbia history, and we can thank the Reverend John Sheepshanks (don't you love that name?) for some great descriptions of life in a raw new country.

The good minister was one of those early Anglican missionaries who left England to administer to the spiritual needs of the new colony, where the magic word "gold" had brought thousands hurrying to seek their fortunes in its rivers and creeks.

In a book published in 1909 entitled *A Bishop in the Rough*, he tells of seeing his new home at New Westminster for the first time in 1859. "Between the prostrate trees and stumps were a few huts, a small collection of wooden stores, some sheds and tents, and a population of perhaps 250 people."

Sheepshanks' first rectory was a draughty log hut, ten feet by seven. The floor was mud and the only window a square hole with a piece of calico across it. It was so cold one winter that the Fraser River froze over. In his rough cabin, Sheepshanks awoke to find the bedclothes near his mouth stiff with ice, and the cups and saucers frozen hard to the shelves in the cupboard.

But it was a joyous time, too. Sleighs were rapidly made, smart with skins and jingling with bells for the ladies to ride in.

"Hockey sticks were cut from the forest, and the male portion of the population—officials, parsons, storekeepers, woodsmen and Indians—engaged in this exciting game upon the broad river," he writes.

New Westminster as it looked in 1863 when it was the capital of the Colony of British Columbia. (COURTESY THE ILLUSTRATED LONDON NEWS.)

Sent up to Barkerville twice during his time in British Columbia, Sheepshanks made the acquaintance of the bloodthirsty mosquito at close quarters as he travelled through the Cariboo. In the wayside houses where he and his companion, the Reverend Robert Dundas, sometimes stayed, he relates:

> There was a ceaseless hum as the room was literally brown with hundreds of mosquitoes. It was swelteringly hot, yet every man wore his coat buttoned up, strings were fastened round his cuffs and trousers. He had gauntlets on his hands, his hat on his head, and a veil hanging down covering his face and neck. He would stick his fork into a piece of meat and pop it in under the veil as quickly as possible. Not a word was spoken. We were too beaten down and cowed by insects.

The Holy Trinity Church, built in 1860 among the stumps at New Westminster. (BCARS A-01672)

Often the wayside inns were mere log hovels. "Wrapped in our blankets, we lay down on the dirty floor along with miners or storekeepers going up or returning from the mines—sometimes carrying their gold dust in belts around their person and a revolver placed conveniently at hand."

One miner caused a nervous flutter to those nearby when he declared, "Wal, mates, I give notice that if I hear anyone moving hereabouts, I shall shoot."

This was before the Cariboo Wagon Road was built, and travel was appalling. The forests were impenetrable, and the hundreds of pack animals going to and from the mines had trampled the trail into a long continuous line of quagmire that "gave forth a sickening stench."

"Day after day we met groups of men, chiefly young Englishmen, turning back, never having reached the mines," wrote Sheepshanks. "Disappointed, broken down, haggard, they cried 'back, back, to go on is madness.'"

Rev. John Sheepshanks.
(BCARS F-05146)

In spite of "mire unspeakable around them, with feet that sunk and slid in the laborious business of walking," the two parsons persevered, and along with their starving horses did indeed reach Barkerville that fall of 1862.

Incidentally, the clerics performed an unusual task in their travels. At that time smallpox was ravaging the native people, so before leaving New Westminster, Sheepshanks obtained some vaccine and a lancet from a doctor attached to the Royal Engineers. At Lake Vert (Green Lake) he inoculated 80 members of a local tribe while sitting on a fallen tree.

"It was a matter of simple faith for the Indians who had never heard of vaccination ... but formed themselves into a line in order of dignity." Later Sheepshanks learned that none had contracted the dread disease.

There was no church at Barkerville when the two parsons arrived, so on the first Sunday evening, Anglican Church services

In the 1860s, wayside inns were mere hovels, and Rev. Sheepshanks was among the many travellers who had to sleep on a dirty floor.
(BCARS D-08238)

were held in the largest drinking saloon in Antler Creek. "The monte tables were swept away, and benches and tables put out for the congregation, and a small table for me," wrote Sheepshanks. "I rang the dinner bell up and down the street ... and soon had a gathering of about thirty men. There was not a woman on the creek."

Although Sheepshanks doesn't mention Williams Lake when recounting their trip through the Cariboo, Dundas, in his journals, singles out the first tiny Williams Lake settlement (in the Glendale area about two to three miles from the present downtown core) as consisting of "sundry small stores and shacks, a log house dignified by the name of Government House, and a wooden jail."

They slept on the floor of the jail and ate at a restaurant run by Marion Woodward, whom Dundas did not like, so on the return trip he was "pleased that a new restaurant had been opened by ex-policeman William Pinchbeck."

Returning to Barkerville again in the spring of 1863, Sheepshanks constructed the first church in the gold fields when he purchased a lot for $500 in Richfield and erected a tiny log cabin church. It held only about a dozen worshippers and the furnishings were very rough, but still it was better than a saloon. (St. Saviour's, the historic Anglican church that still dominates the main street at Barkerville, was not opened until 1870.)

It is doubtful those early visits of the clergy had any great effect on the primitive gold camp where gambling, drinking, and prostitution were a way of life for the lonely and depressed miners. Often the parsons were ridiculed and their sermons interrupted with jokes and rude comments.

On his way back to New Westminster, Sheepshanks stopped at the 141 Mile wayside house and "found himself on the track of a great crime." Tom Clegg, a young Wells Fargo expressman who was carrying a considerable consignment of gold, had been murdered just 48 hours before when he and his friend were jumped by two men on the trail south of the house.

"The murder was followed by a long chase of many days and nights. The country was in a state of excitement for the little expressman was very popular." One of the murderers drowned while trying to cross the Bonaparte River, while the other was captured, tried, and hanged at Lillooet. (See *Cariboo-Chilcotin Pioneer People and Places* for the full story.)

Early in the summer of 1864 the young parson left British Columbia, and over the next three years he embarked on another incredible journey that would see him travelling across the United States and on to the West Indies, Hawaii, Asia, and Russia.

Returning home to England, he later became the Bishop of Norwich and in 1908 wrote the remarkable book on his experiences.

The Story of Chief Anahim

by Benny Jack

This is the story of Chief Anahim, as my grand-father, Old Stillas, told it to me many years ago. As a little boy I heard about the people who lived in this country before us.

Chief Anahim, a Bella Coola Indian, lived on the coast where his forefathers fished the waters at the foot of the mountains. His people, the Kwakiutl, lived to the north in the valleys that drain into the waters of the Pacific.

Several times each year there were occasions to celebrate. A potlatch would bring together Chief Anahim's people and the Bella Coola tribe. They came from the north and from the south to Bella Coola village to mourn the dead, to honour the great, to hold council, to feast, to dance, and to carry on their ancient and traditional rituals.

Indeed, Bella Coola was a good place in which to live—between the sea that yielded its fish and the mountains that gave their protection. The trees stood tall and proud—as tall and as proud as the log houses and totems in the villages by the seaside. The winters were long and wet, and the mist hung heavy in the valleys.

Chief Anahim had eyes for a woman who did not belong to his people. She had been raised in the rugged Chilcotin country. Chief Anahim married her and brought her to Bella Coola.

Bella Coola was not like the Chezacut, where she had been brought up. The land along the coast was misty and moist. She disliked the endless days of rain and the gloomy darkness among the tall trees. She was unhappy, and with her strong mind she persuaded her husband to move out of this part of the country.

The whole band followed them. They crossed the mountains and came to live at Anahim Lake. There the sky was high and wide. The air was crisp and the frosty ground did not allow much to grow. Even Chief Anahim had not found the land without blemish. His catches were not as great as the wealth of fish had promised. The lake would not give away its riches.

One day Chief Anahim's wife heard about better and richer land. The Shuswap Indians used to make their homes there. There grass would grow thicker and taller for their horses and cows. They would reap what they had sown—a good harvest from a good land.

Again Chief Anahim agreed to move. The whole band came to live near Alexis Creek. There, at last, Anahim's wife found the country she liked. She called her new home "The Anahim Rancheree."

Benny Jack was an Ulkatcho Carrier Indian from Anahim Lake who worked as a researcher for the Ulkatcho Band and developed a deep interest in the history of his people. The story of Chief Anahim is just one of the stories he produced before his death in February 1978 at age 38.

Benny Jack. (COURTESY BRENDA CAHOOSE)

Indian Fish Trap

A fence or weir was built across a narrow part of a lake or river, and these basket traps were set into the fence. The remains of one such fence could still be seen near the public campground on little Anahim Lake until recent years according to Thomas Squinas, son of the late Chief Squinas, and other Indian residents.

The Anahim Lake area was, and still is, called Nakwuntl'u in the local language. The name turns up frequently in the reports and maps of early explorers and surveyors of the area during the nineteenth century.

—Benny Jack

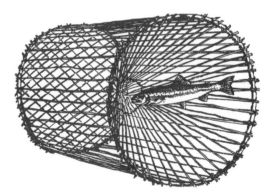

A fish trap of the type used in the Anahim Lake area in Chief Anahim's time over a century ago. (DRAWING BY B.J. JACK)

He Lost a Wager and Won a Ranch

by Clive Stangoe

In 1994, two Chilcotin ranches that have been owned and operated for 100 years or more by the same families were presented with Century Ranch and Farm awards by the Ministry of Agriculture. Honoured were the Durrell family of the Wineglass Ranch at Riske Creek (see page 141), and the Bayliff family of the Chilancoh Ranch near Redstone.

In the fall of 1886 a young Englishman reined in his horse on a bluff overlooking the verdant Chilcotin River valley near Redstone and decided this was the place where he wanted to set down roots.

A century later those roots are still deep, as the fourth generation of Bayliffs continues to operate the historic Chilancoh Ranch.

The founder, Hugh Peel Bayliff, was only eighteen when he immigrated to British Columbia, working first for the Cornwall brothers at Ashcroft, then at the Cherry Creek Ranch near Kamloops. He was delivering a string of horses to the Ulkatcho for Tom Hance when he got his first glimpse of the vast Chilcotin in all its autumn splendour.

He was back early in '87 and pre-empted 160 acres near Redstone, then returned to Cherry Creek for his first 100 heifers, which he brought overland via the Gang Ranch, swimming them across the Fraser and Chilcotin rivers, dangerously swollen in the spring freshet. He also brought along friend Norman Lee, another English immigrant.

Chilancoh founder Hugh Bayliff on his favourite saddle horse, Strayshot, in front of his first home.

Hugh Bayliff was destined to be a successful rancher. Strong and well built, this son of an English clergyman was a magnificent horseman and an avid outdoorsman with a sure knowledge of handling cattle. His brand, the Bar Eleven, was the first one registered in the upper Chilcotin.

The first few years of establishing himself at Redstone were busy and exciting times for Bayliff. He built a solid log home, took Lee in as partner, got married, lost a wager, and ended up sole owner of the Chilancoh.

When the two bachelors became partners, they made an unusual agreement: when one of them married, they would toss a coin to see who would buy the other out. In 1891 when Bayliff returned from England with bride Gertrude Tyndle, the partners tossed—and Hugh lost. Lee was unable to come up with the money, however, so in the end Bayliff won and the ranch stayed in the family.

Despite her gentle upbringing, Gertrude quickly adapted to the isolation and primitive life, and with her medical knowledge and skilled horsemanship she was a great

Gertrude Bayliff rode sidesaddle and helped with cattle roundups.

asset to the community. Riding sidesaddle, she helped with cattle roundups and won many trophies at the races on Becher's Prairie at Riske Creek, riding her own racehorses.

The Bayliff ranch as it looked in the late 1800s. Most of the old buildings have disappeared, and today's modern ranch is now surrounded by trees.

The Chilcotin River valley near Redstone was, at the turn of the century, a small enclave of English families. Among them was Reginald Newton, who ranched nearby and raised polo ponies. Bayliff took to the game like the proverbial duck to water and

Hugh and Gertrude Bayliff dressed for dinner.

became an outstanding player. A field on the Bayliff property is still referred to as the polo field, and a scuffed polo ball is one of the ornaments in the present Bayliff home, along with a silver rose bowl won by the Bayliff team three years running.

The Bayliff family also brought a touch of Edwardian England into their home. On the outside the plain log building was the picture of spartan frontier life, but inside there was an air of the Old Country. The logs had been sheathed; dark panelling around the lower half was offset by white plaster above. Drapes drawn in the evening hid the reality of a rugged country from view, and the family always dressed for dinner, sitting down to a table set with silver and fine china.

During the years 1919 to 1925, Hugh Bayliff built a new two-storey home with lumber sawn on his own small mill, which is now on display at Fort Langley's Agricultural Museum. Every piece of finish lumber was planed by hand. Without insulation, frame houses can be decidedly chilly in Chilcotin winters, but Bayliff had the walls covered with five layers of rough lumber so that even today it remains a comfortable retreat when January winds howl down the valley.

In preparing for the project, Bayliff bought a steel-wheeled Fordson tractor in Kamloops and drove it back home. He would later remark that the "slow jolting ride resulted in every rock along the way being imprinted on my posterior."

Hugh and Gertrude's only son, Gabriel "Gay" Thomas Bayliff, was

Second-generation rancher Gabriel "Gay" Bayliff.

married in the "new" house in 1923 to English-born Dorothy Dyson. The couple had met in England where Gay attended school, and Dorothy subsequently made several trips to the Chilcotin to visit her uncle, Reginald Newton.

The young English transplant flourished in the Chilcotin. Like many ranch wives, she rode in cattle roundups, helped with haying, and prepared meals for crews that sometimes numbered sixteen men. And she did it all with the charm and quiet dignity that seems to be the hallmark of the Bayliff women.

When he took over the 3,000-acre Chilancoh Ranch after his father's death in 1934, Gay concentrated on building up the herd of straight-bred Hereford cattle. Active in beef circles, he was a well-known figure in the industry until his death in 1977.

Gay and Dorothy had two sons, Tim and Tony. Both have remained to ranch in the Chilcotin—Tim with the Chilancoh, and Tony at the nearby Newton Ranch. Over the years that Tim Bayliff was at the family helm, he maintained the same efficient operation his father and grandfather were noted for. A former president of the B.C. Cattlemen's Association, he is still well known and respected in the beef industry.

Tim carried on with the English connection when in 1954 he married Merle Glenny of Somerset, a nurse at the Alexis Creek Outport Hospital. The couple had three children—Hugh, Elizabeth,

*Tim Bayliff (left - Irene Stangoe photo) and Hugh Bayliff Jr., third-
and fourth-generation ranchers respectively.*

and James. Elizabeth is a lawyer practising in Prince George;
unfortunately Jim was killed in a logging accident in 1994.

Hugh, the eldest, named for the great-grandfather who pre-
empted that first 160 acres overlooking the Chilcotin River so long
ago, is now carrying on with the Bayliff tradition, taking the
Chilancoh Ranch with its 55,000 deeded acres and 800 head of
cattle into its second century.

(All uncredited photos courtesy of Tim Bayliff.)

Fort Chilcotin

Although there is nothing to mark its existence today, a modest log structure once dominated the field above the junction of the Chilcotin and Chilco Rivers just a few miles from the Bayliff ranch house. It was the site of Fort Chilcotin, one of the many Hudson's Bay Company forts that dotted the north country known as New Caledonia.

Established in 1829, it was abandoned a number of times over the years, due partly to its isolation but mainly to the hostility of the Chilcotin Indians, who could rarely be persuaded to bring in their furs to trade.

Although the fort closed permanently in 1844, it was still destined to play an important role in Cariboo-Chilcotin history.

In 1864, Chilcotin natives massacred thirteen white men working on the Waddington Trail, an ambitious scheme to find a shorter route to the Cariboo gold fields overland from Bute Inlet. There are many possible explanations for the sudden uprising, ranging from the white man's introduction of smallpox and the theft of Indian land to starvation and the abuse of Indian women.

Gold Commissioner W.G. Cox headed one of the armed patrols sent out by Governor Frederick Seymour to track down the wanted men. After months of relentless pursuit, eight Indians headed by Chief Klatassine decided to meet with Cox at the camp he had set up in the deserted Fort Chilcotin. They hoped to find a peaceful solution to their "war." They were immediately arrested. Five of the men were later hanged at Quesnel.

The old fort remained Hudson's Bay Company property until the 1930s, when the Bayliff family purchased it. In later years, Chilcotin old-timer Bill Bliss told of seeing arrowheads and shreds of HBC money on the site.

Barkerville Tales

Stories abound about the historic gold-rush town of Barkerville: the fortunes that were made and lost; the indescribable conditions under which the miners laboured, always hoping to strike the "big one;" and the fabulous characters who peopled its muddy streets, many of whom stayed to die in this raw land called the Cariboo.

There are some light-hearted stories of Barkerville, too, including this joke, which appeared in the *Tribune* on February 2, 1933.

> He was a sad-eyed prospector and he arrived with his pack at the Pearly Gates with the fond hope of his heavenly reward for a life well spent. St. Peter shook his grey head, saying, "Sorry, old top, but we're full up; not even standing room."
>
> "Gosh all fish-hooks," exclaimed the old gold hunter, "but I'm a prospector from the Cariboo."
>
> "Too bad," replied St. Peter, "but there's hundreds of Cariboo prospectors in here right now. I guess you will have to wait outside a while."
>
> "Wait a minute," shouted the prospector, "just nail this notice up on them there pearly gates," and he hastily scribbled the following:
>
> ### BIG GOLD STRIKE REPORTED
> ### AT BARKERVILLE
> ### BEST FIND IN FIFTY YEARS
>
> St. Peter posted the sign, and shortly after, a stream of old prospectors crowded out from heaven, bound for Barkerville.

"Alright," said St. Peter, " you can come in now. There's lots of room."

The old chap hesitated, eyed the open gates, looked after the departing crowd, then resolutely shouldered his pack again.

"Nope," he declared, "guess I'll maybe see you later. There may be something in that durn rumour after all."

W.G.R Hinds' 1864 painting captures the mood of the gold rush and the characters infected by the gold fever that kept men always searching and dreaming. (Courtesy McCord Museum)

B.C.'s First Boxing Champion

Did you know that the first boxing championship in British Columbia was held at Barkerville in 1867?

And what a fight it must have been for the 1,500 spectators who crowded into the gold-rush camp to watch the event, clustering on the slopes or climbing trees to get a good view. According to the *Cariboo Sentinel*, betting was lively with some $12,000 changing hands long before the two boxers—George Wilson, 33, and Joe Eden, 27—took their places in the 24-foot makeshift outdoor ring.

The two bully boys were stripped to the waist, and immediately started belabouring each other with unprotected fists. Although all the known rules of boxing were carefully observed, the fights were often extremely violent and many injuries were sustained.

The fight went twenty rounds, and the referee and support teams kept out of the ring to avoid being hurt. The blood ran red, and in

Prize Fight

in Barkerville

> **CHALLENGE**
>
> THE UNDERSIGEND HEREBY CHALLENGES
> ANY man in British Columbia or Vancouver Island,
> irrespective of nationality or color, to fight a FAIR
> PRIZE FIGHT, according to the rules of English
> P.R., for $2,000 a side. If Mr. George Baker means
> to fight he will leave an opportunity of doing so by
> accepting this challenge, and if not from hence-
> forth stop his gassing. Articles and a deposit will be
> ready to Tom Barry's Saloon, Cameronton, next
> Saturday Evening.
>
> **GEORGE WILSON**
> **Williams Creek, 6th August, 1866**

Advertisement in the Cariboo Sentinel.

the emergency bars set up just outside the melee, the whiskey ran like sparkling gold.

Eden led off, planting a stinger on Wilson's left peeper. In the second round he revealed his strategy of hitting a good blow, then "falling" to the ground to avoid retaliation, as the rules restricted a fighter from abusing a downed opponent. He did this in the third round and in the fourth, fifth, and sixth rounds until Wilson lost his temper. While Eden was falling in the seventh, Wilson managed to get a headlock on him, administered some well-directed blows, and at the same time wrung his neck thoroughly.

Not enough to kill him, apparently, as the fight went on. In the last round Eden connected with a severe blow to Wilson's midriff, and as he "went to grass" (fell) as usual, Wilson struck him. Wilson then lost the fight on this foul.

The *Cariboo Sentinel* editorialized that "Wilson fought for glory while Eden fought for money." His purse was $1,000.

There Were Scoundrels in Those Days

Now for a bit more humour from the *Cariboo Sentinel*, which had no hesitation in calling a scoundrel a scoundrel, libel and slander laws be damned.

If a man was a swindler, cheat, or drunkard, he was often exposed in a paid advertisement in the *Sentinel*. For instance, it didn't hesitate to name Lawyer Parker when he was ejected from the gold commissioner's court three times while drunk.

And when James Hood skipped town owing money, it published this letter dated August 18, 1865, from merchant James Dalgetty:

> Last week when you left Williams Lake Creek with around $12,000 in your pocket which you made this year as a shareholder in the Erickson Claim, you promised to pay me the $360 you owe me.
>
> Unfortunately I took you for an honest man and accepted your word, but that evening you went off clandestinely ... .

Dalgetty goes on to say that unless Hood sends the money, a "card" will be sent for publication in the *San Francisco Bulletin*, the *Forces Gazette*, and the *Moresby Advertiser*, so that "your father and your friends in your native place may see how you have acted to a countryman who befriended you when you had not a cent to call your own."

Instead of suing for defamation of character, Hood inserted an advertisement in the *Sentinel* announcing he had settled with Dalgetty and had even overpaid the bill by $25.

The owner of the *Sentinel* had his own way of dealing with merchants who owed the newspaper money; he printed their advertisements upside down!

Justice appears to have been so much easier and swifter in those days.

Beaver Lake
Stopping House

Right up until her death in January 1995 at 92 years of age, Ethel Hamilton was a walking encyclopaedia of Cariboo history and often regaled me with tales of the Beaver Lake stopping house that was her home for most of her life.

Ethel's mother was Christine "Toppy" Eagle, who was born at the Onward Ranch that her father, Charles B. Eagle, had acquired near the head of Williams Lake in 1867.

"When my grandfather Eagle died, he left his five children $8,000 each," said Ethel. "My Uncle Willie [Eagle] then bought the Beaver Lake Ranch and talked my mother into letting him look after her $8,000 too."

"But Uncle Willie was a real dude and blew the money," Ethel related. Later, feeling some remorse, he turned the ranch over to his sister before going away to fight in the Boer War. Willie died in South Africa in 1908, not from war injuries, but from the terrible wounds he suffered when attacked by lions (see *Looking Back at the Cariboo-Chilcotin*).

Ethel's father also came from pioneer stock. Gavin Hamilton Sr., who was Hudson's Bay factor at Fort St. James, moved to 150 Mile in 1878 and later settled at Lac la Hache. His son, Gavin Jr., first saw Toppy Eagle when he went to work at the Onward Ranch. "She was a pretty thing and he watched her growing up," said Ethel. They fell in love, were married in 1899 at St. Joseph's Mission, then went to live at Beaver Lake.

In gold-rush days, Beaver Lake was an important stopping place on the many trails leading to the riches in the Cariboo Mountains.

Gavin Hamilton Jr. and his wife Christine, known as "Toppy."
(COURTESY ETHEL HAMILTON)

Among the early settlers was packer Francois "Frank" Guy, who in 1870, with his associate Ah Tom, bought the flourishing Beaver Lake roadhouse and store owned by Jim Sellars and Peter Dunlevy (generally credited with starting the great Cariboo gold rush with his strike on the Horsefly River in 1859).

In 1896 Guy decided to build a new house near the original roadhouse. Known as Guy's House, this was the home later acquired by Willie Eagle, then by Toppy and her husband.

The young Hamiltons soon added on to the small house and made it into a large, comfortable roadside inn with a big living-room and a mirror-lined bar with brass rail downstairs, and five bedrooms upstairs. Ethel could recall the big iron stoves, brought in in pieces by pack horse, which heated the rooms; the Chinese cooks carrying buckets of water suspended from a wooden yoke on their shoulders; and the noise of men playing cards and drinking in the bar. She spoke of the big freight wagons with their ten- and twelve-horse teams that were a familiar sight pulling into the yard.

One of Ethel's most prized possessions was a set of three heavy ledgers dating from 1899 to 1910 in which were recorded the many transactions at Beaver Lake House. Many pioneer names written in a beautiful script dot the pages: Pablo Tresierra, William Laing Meason, Louis Crosina, John Murphy, Alex Meiss, William Parker, Fred Rose,

E.J. Patenaude, James Murphy, Sandy McInnis. The words NO LIQUOR appear in bold letters after Chinese and Indian names.

And these were some of the prices: "A bottle of rye cost $1.25; fifteen pounds of beef, $1.50; eight pounds of tallow, 75 cents; a tin of salmon, 25 cents; cigarettes, 50 cents; gloves, 75 cents; a loaf of bread, 25 cents." Teamsters could get a meal and night's lodging for $1.50, with 50 cents for each horse.

Ethel Hamilton in later years.
(COURTESY TISSIE NELSON)

The hard-working Hamiltons had a huge garden and sold vegetables, but most of their groceries came up once a year from Harvey Bailey's store at Ashcroft, or from the 153 Mile Store. No Williams Lake village then. Ethel's father also ran a small sawmill and cut ties for the Pacific Great Eastern Railway when it was being pushed up through the Cariboo.

Ethel was born at Lac la Hache, the second eldest of the nine Hamilton children, and at the time of my interview in 1994, this bright feisty lady was the only one of her family left.

Her memories took her back to those early years when she travelled by sleigh or stagecoach to attend St. Ann's Academy at Kamloops, stopping every fifteen miles at wayside houses so the four-horse teams could be changed. And when Williams Lake came into being in 1919, she thought nothing of riding her horse the 35-mile journey into the village to go "stampeding."

Ethel never married but led a busy, colourful life as a cook in many of the pioneer hotels in the Cariboo, eventually returning to her beloved Beaver Lake. She was living there in February 1971 with two of her brothers when fire broke out in an upstairs room and destroyed the old stopping house, marking the end of another chapter in Cariboo-Chilcotin history.

The Beaver Lake House with its mirror-lined bar was a favourite stopping place for teamsters on their way to and from Quesnel Forks.
(COURTESY ETHEL HAMILTON)

Beaver Lake House,

On the Main Line between 150 Mile House and Quesnel Forks

Good accommodations for travelers
Good stabling, feed, etc, for teams.
A well stocked Bar in connection
Dealers in Hay, Grain, and Produce.

EAGLE & HAMILTON, Prop's.

An 1899 advertisement.

Making Bread in the Good Old Days

Many people today have bread-making machines. You dump in some water; add flour, yeast, sugar, butter, and milk; punch a couple of buttons; and voila! In a couple of hours out comes a beautiful loaf of bread.

It wasn't so easy back in "the good old days."

The travelling correspondent for the *Victoria Daily Colonist* who visited the Pinchbeck and Lyne ranch at Williams Lake in 1886 was obviously impressed by the magnificence of the farm, which then encompassed the entire valley.

"To walk over the farm would be too great an effort, so Mr. Pinchbeck harnessed up a team and drove us from one end to the other," he wrote. William Pinchbeck and William Lyne had been in partnership at Williams Lake since the 1860s and now had acres and acres sown to wheat and barley, hundreds of head of cattle grazing on their vast property, as well as innumerable hogs and horses, a huge vegetable garden, a brick-kiln, distillery, and brewery. For many years, however, they hauled their grain by horse-drawn wagon to a mill (likely the one at Soda Creek, built in 1867) to be ground into flour.

That all changed in 1885 when the enterprising partners bought a flour mill at Victoria, then dismantled and packed it in to the Cariboo by mule train. The massive 600-pound millstones imported from France were five feet in diameter and held together by metal bands.

The year before, Pinchbeck had made a trip back to the Old Country and returned with an English bride, a steam thresher, and

This large flour mill once dominated the Williams Lake Creek valley just upstream from the BC Rail depot. Above it is the grain warehouse and the miller's house, right. (VANCOUVER CITY ARCHIVES)

a sawmill. When the Victoria correspondent visited, the thresher was "doing its work in a lively manner," and the sacks of grain were then taken the short distance to the mill to be ground into flour.

"The mill is very substantially built and we were shown some excellent samples of flour," he wrote. "The wheat here has been given the highest honors obtainable in the world at the Colonial Exhibition in London."

Pinchbeck's niece Emma also accompanied him back to the Cariboo from England, and years later she would remember the great water system her uncle built for the enormous ranch. "He had a wing-dam in Williams Lake Creek and a huge water wheel that raised the water into a flume. I know that in a very dry season one year, he dammed up water in Lac la Hache and Williams Lake to get power for the flour mill."

Her most vivid memory, however, was of the water system in the kitchen. "There was a flume that ran into a water barrel under the sink in the kitchen floor, and we used to dip water from this barrel into the sink. Often the

The Soda Creek flour mill, one of the earliest in the Cariboo, ceased operations in 1942. (BCARS E-02135)

WILLIAMS
LAKE MILLS
No. ONE
BAKERS
⚜ EXTRA FLOUR ⚜
Put up by
Wm PINCHBECK.

Flour from the Williams Lake mill was put up in sacks of unbleached cotton that were printed with this illustration after William Pinchbeck (right) became the sole owner of the ranch. (BCARS F-04381)

frogs used to jump out of the flume onto the kitchen floor and into the sink."

I couldn't establish the exact date the Williams Lake mill ceased operations. The Pinchbeck/Lyne partnership was dissolved in 1888, and when Pinchbeck died in 1893, heavily mortgaged to the Gang Ranch, most of his holdings were sold at auction. Possibly the mill machinery was included. Certainly by 1912, when the Pacific Great Eastern Railway purchased the ranch for the new townsite of Williams Lake, the flour mill would have been finished.

Local old-timers Wilf Moore, Colin Curtis, and Olive (Lock) McKenzie all remember climbing around the old building as youngsters in the late 1920s. "It was just a shell then and rather dangerous," remembered Olive. All agreed that sometime after that it was torn down. The grinding stones, the last vestiges to remain, were retrieved from the creek in 1947 and can be seen today at the Tourist Information Centre.

The history of flour milling in the Cariboo goes way back to fur brigade days, when a small mill was established in 1843 by the Hudson's Bay Company at Fort Alexandria to provide flour for its staff and the many travellers who stopped at the big fort.

The first flour mill on the mainland built by private enterprise, however, was established at Dog Creek in 1861 by a couple of colourful pioneers—Samuel Leander Charles "Charlie" Brown and his partner Le Comte de Versepuche, later known as Gaspard.

According to legend, the Count left his Paris home to replenish the family fortunes, first trying his luck in the California gold fields, then in 1860 heading for the Cariboo. Ending up at Dog Creek, he soon traded his elaborate tri-cornered hat and blue satin jacket worn at the court of Louis XVI to Chilcotin Chief Alexis for a tidy band of sturdy horses.

A miller at Santa Fe, New Mexico, Charlie Brown headed for California in 1849, then the Cariboo, where he soon became known as one of the best packers in the country. Although he was

S.L.C. "Charlie" Brown and his partner established the first flour mill to be built on the mainland by private enterprise at Dog Creek.
(BCARS G-09462)

a small man, it's said he packed in all the machinery and boilers for the sternwheeler *Enterprise*, which was being built near Fort Alexandria, as well as four billiard tables for the Hotel de France at Barkerville, for which he got paid $4,000 in gold dust.

Settling at Dog Creek, he and Versepuche began constructing a grist mill, even though they were ridiculed for believing wheat would grow in such a raw, primitive land. By the following year their Pioneer Mill was into production. It got a bad name for producing poor flour at first, but within a year or so was turning out a very good article indeed. The mill was acquired in 1886 by Joseph Place, who later moved the stones and machinery closer to the creek, erected a new building and water wheel, and continued to grind

The original Dog Creek mill.

grain until 1924. Today the big water wheel, a millstone, and some tumbledown timbers are all that remain.

Following the success at Dog Creek, it didn't take long for two flour mills to be built at Lillooet. Although Williams Lake was touted as a possible site for another interior mill by 1866, Soda Creek was chosen—probably because it was one of the busiest stopping places on the Cariboo Wagon Road. Here stagecoaches and freight wagons met the sternwheelers that transported passengers and goods upriver to Quesnel and thus on to Barkerville. It would be another twenty years before Pinchbeck and Lyne established their own mill at Williams Lake.

In its first year (1867), the Soda Creek mill turned out 70,000 pounds of flour and was proving a great boon to Barkerville, where the price of flour dropped drastically—from $1.50 per pound to seven cents. It was probably not surprising that another mill was built at Deep Creek, a short distance away, a year later. Called the Protection Mill, it was dismantled in 1916. The Soda Creek mill, which closed in 1942, was the last of the early colonial mills to operate in the Cariboo. The stones are on display at the museum in Williams Lake.

There were other flour mills operating throughout the Cariboo in the early years, of course—at Quesnel and Clinton—and later ranchers at places like Hanceville, Springhouse, and 150 Mile House built small mills for their own use. Some produced good flour and some, well, not so good.

There are two theories about why the flour mills disappeared. First, huge roller mills were introduced on the prairies that could manufacture a better quality flour at a much lower price; and secondly, the coming of the PGE Railway meant that flour could be brought in relatively easily and cheaply.

By the early 1920s, all the necessary ingredients to make a loaf of bread in the Williams Lake area could be picked up at Mackenzies Ltd. or the T.A. Moore store, which brings my story full circle ... almost. It would be another 75 years before we got home bread-making machines.

The 150 Mile Hotel

Most people passing the 150 Mile Hotel today will not realize that hidden behind its modern facade is one of the oldest buildings in the Cariboo, dating back over 100 years to a time when stagecoaches and freight wagons lumbered past its doors.

Originally a home built in the late 1800s by Gavin Hamilton Sr., it was later known as the "doctor's house" before it finally became a hotel. Even today the little lake behind it is still known as Doctor's Lake.

Hamilton, a retired Hudson's Bay Company factor from Fort St. James, purchased the 150 Mile Ranch and store in 1878, taking up residence with his wife Margaret and their fifteen children in the big 150 Mile stopping house, built in the early 1860s during the first frantic gold-rush days. I can only surmise that he later built the smaller home a bit farther south for some of his large family.

Adversity dogged Hamilton in his new venture. Fire destroyed his sawmill and a storehouse one year, then a creek overflowed, wiping out some of his acreage. Finally, overwhelmed by debt, he sold to the firm of Vieth and Borland in 1883 and moved to Lac la Hache.

At that time the 150 Mile House was still a bustling junction on the Cariboo Wagon Road. Passengers, freight, and mail made connections here for way-points north and east, while others headed west to the Chilcotin by way of the Onward Ranch, then down the Chimney Creek valley to cross the Fraser River by scow.

But although there was lots of activity, there wasn't much in the way of medical help at the 150 Mile House. There was no Williams

Lake village then, remember, so the sick had to make a long and arduous trip by stagecoach to the hospital at either Ashcroft or Barkerville.

That changed in 1896 when the first registered full-time doctor arrived to set up his office and home in the former Hamilton house. He was Dr. R.T. Wilson Herald, a handsome 35-year-old practitioner with a sweeping moustache, who over the next four years could often be seen travelling by horse and buggy to minister to his patients throughout the Cariboo. He was followed by Dr. Mostyn Hoops, then Dr. Cecil Boyd, and it was undoubtedly during these years that the Hamilton house became known as the doctor's house.

Dr. R.T. Wilson Herald.
(COURTESY JOHN ROBERTS)

In 1915 the doctor's house became the home of pioneer trucker Tommy Hodgson and bride Edythe Paxton, but in 1920, when the young couple moved into the new Williams Lake village, the doctor's house was converted into a hotel. By this time the original 150 Mile roadhouse, where Gavin Hamilton and his family had lived and catered to travellers from all walks of life, was gone—destroyed by fire in 1916.

Sonia (Cowan) Cornwall, who has lived in the 150 Mile area most of her life, can remember as a youngster dreading her visits to the hotel in the 1920s to see Dr. Sumner, a travelling dentist, who would set up his chair in the front parlour. "Those waiting their turn sat around the room and watched. It was awful."

Long-time 150 Mile storeowner Clarence Zirnhelt was even more graphic. "The drill was worked with long belts and strings and was pumped by his foot. Sometimes the drill would get stuck in your tooth, and of course there was no anaesthetic."

From 1912 to 1928 the 150 Mile Ranch and townsite were owned by an English syndicate known as the Cariboo Trading Company, then were acquired by Charles Cowan, owner of the nearby Onward Ranch. He hired Maude Cornwall, a well-known Cariboo cook, to manage the hotel for him. A beer licence (probably the first) issued in 1924 in Maude's name was still on the wall many years later.

Hauling ice blocks from Doctor's Lake in the 1940s. That's Betty McKenzie at the reins.
(COURTESY BETTY MCKENZIE KOWALSKI)

In 1939 Zirnhelt took over management of the hotel and brought in Maggie Hamilton, Gavin's daughter, as manager. "She was a great cook," he reminisced, "but put up too good a table." At fifty cents a meal, Clarence was often in the hole.

Times were tough during the war years, Clarence recalled. Sometimes only one or two people a night would come through. "We would leave the register in the hallway, and those coming in late would just sign their name, pick up a key, and help themselves to a room." The rate was $2.50 a night. He eventually had to close for a few years.

In 1945 Zirnhelt sub-leased the hotel to Ken and Barbara McKenzie, whose daughter, Betty Kowalski, still talks fondly of their years at the 150 Hotel, despite the hard work. "My folks bought and raised 5,000 chicks in the spring. Every morning 25 would be butchered for lunch, then in the afternoon another 25 for dinner."

The 150 Mile Hotel, formerly the doctor's house, as it looked in 1930, still shaded by the giant cottonwoods. (BCARS B-04930)

Pigs had to be fed, cows milked, butter churned, and laundry done on a gas-powered washing machine. Her dad also cut 200 blocks of ice from Doctor's Lake each winter, using a cross-cut saw and hauling them by team and wagon to a nearby shed to be covered with sawdust.

The McKenzies stayed for six years. When Cowan died, Druscilla (Cowan) Hodgson inherited the hotel from her dad's estate, but immediately ran into new regulations for hotel and beer parlours. "You had to have so many rooms, half with baths, and so many square feet, so I had to add on."

That meant that the giant cottonwoods in front of the hotel, a landmark for many years, had to be cut down. "Maggie Hamilton was pretty upset with me as she had planted them as a child," Dru recalled, "but there was nowhere else to build."

Under a share arrangement with Howe Construction Co., which did the renovations, the old 150 Mile Hotel soon blossomed with a handsome addition, complete with a beer parlour and restaurant and sixteen rooms upstairs, including those in the doctor's house, which had vanished from view behind the smart new facade.

The old/new hotel has had many owners since then. In 1991 it was purchased by the present owner, Michael Procter, who is proud of the historic part of his hotel, which he believes ranks as one of the oldest in the province. Although the original sitting room is now the beer cooler, and the rock fireplace that once warmed many a traveller is boarded up and hidden behind plywood, evidence of Gavin Hamilton's original house can still be found upstairs, where the chimney incongruously thrusts up right through the middle of the corridor—a reminder of the good old days when it radiated heat to the seven little bedrooms.

And it still sits on the original rock foundation laid down over 100 years ago.

Shorty Dunn and
the Grey Fox

The life and times of the notorious Bill Miner, the American bandit known as the Grey Fox, have been well documented in books, films, and on television. But little has been told of his accomplice, William "Shorty" Dunn, and his brief sojourn in the Cariboo.

According to the late Enid Wright and her son Wilfred, whom I interviewed at their 132 Mile Ranch in 1985, a field just eight miles east of their historic home was named the Billy Dunn Meadow after the prospector-turned-robber.

Shorty reputedly lived in a log cabin at the meadow for a year or two before taking part in the famous CPR train robbery at Ducks (now called Monte Creek), sixteen miles east of Kamloops, which was masterminded by Miner in 1906.

But this was not Shorty's first holdup. He was prospecting in the Princeton area when he first met the soft-spoken George Edwards (alias Bill Miner), and they soon became friends.

In September 1904, when Bill Miner staged his first Canadian train robbery, holding up the CPR at Mission and escaping with $7,000 in gold dust and $50,000 in U.S. Bonds, one of his two partners in crime was Shorty Dunn.

Despite the combined efforts of the famed Pinkerton Detective Agency from the U.S. and the B.C. Police, they were never caught for this crime. Most historical references contend that Miner and Dunn both returned to the Princeton area, where they led exemplary lives, quietly ranching and prospecting.

Not so, according to the Wrights. They believe that Shorty was "hiding out" in the meadow near the 132 Mile House, waiting for the heat to die down. Two years later he helped Miner pull the Kamloops job, which incidentally netted them only $15 and a bottle of liver pills.

When Shorty was caught, along with Miner and another accomplice, Louis Colquhoun, Cariboo residents could not believe he was guilty, said the Wrights, and a petition was circulated throughout the area asking people to vouch for his good character.

The petition had little effect. Along with Miner, Shorty was convicted and sentenced to life imprisonment in the B.C. Penitentiary at New Westminster. Miner had spent a

William "Shorty" Dunn. (BCARS B-09643)

lifetime robbing stagecoaches and trains and had escaped from American prisons many times over the years, so it probably came as no surprise when he was able to break out of the New Westminster pen just a year later.

Despite his life of crime, the tall slim bandit was a gentle, polite man, fond of children and highly regarded in communities like Merritt and Princeton where he lived under his alias George Edwards. He died a folk hero in a Georgia prison in 1913. Colquhoun was sent to prison at Walla Walla and died there of tuberculosis.

Short, stocky Bill Dunn appears to have been well liked in the Cariboo, although one article describes him as "surly and decidedly slow." Shorty did his time at the B.C. Pen until 1918, when he was paroled. He then moved to Ootsa Lake in central B.C. where he lived until his death by drowning in 1927.

And One for the Road ...

I wonder what would happen today if a couple of bank clerks carrying money satchels were found passed out by the side of the road? One could imagine all kinds of dire consequences, not the least of which would be the loss of their jobs.

But escapades like that were fairly common occurrences back in 1919 and 1920, when clerks would ride up from the Bank of Montreal at the 150 Mile House to the new village of Williams Lake with the payroll money for the Pacific Great Eastern Railway workers. The trials and tribulations they encountered in those prohibition days due to bootleggers and the demon rum seem unbelievable today.

At that time 150 Mile House was an old, well-established centre, and the Bank of Montreal occupied a large two-storey white building beside Borland Creek just south of the bridge. When Williams Lake sprang into being in 1919 with the building of the PGE, the B of M immediately opened a subagency in the new village in a rough tarpaper shack across the tracks, giving service from the 150 Mile branch twice a week.

On one particular occasion, so the story goes, the clerk felt it necessary to ready himself for the ten-mile horseback trip up to Williams Lake with several bottles of liquid refreshment. As he jogged along, he stopped the horse every now and again for a rest, so that by the time he reached Williams Lake he was well under the influence.

The inebriated lad managed to get to the new Fraser and Mackenzie store on Railway Avenue, and there, unbeknownst to the staff, he crawled under a counter to sleep off the effects of his travels. But somehow, on his wayward path, he had managed to drop the money bag beside the road, where it was later found by some good-natured townspeople. Locating the clerk still under the store counter, sleeping, blissfully unaware of his little oversight, they carefully placed the money under his head and covered him with blankets. Payday didn't come until the next morning.

The first Bank of Montreal in Williams Lake, a subagency of the main 150 Mile branch, was housed in this shack built in 1919.

Then there's the story told by early resident Ethel Slater, whose husband Walter would become the first liquor vendor in Williams Lake in 1921. It was the first time that clerks H. Campbell and Murdo MacKenzie had brought up the payroll from the 150 Mile—about $3,000, she wrote. "They met up with Pat Hoy, the flourishing bootlegger, and staggered around together until they passed out by old Bob Henderson's store near the Stampede grounds. Bob went to the rescue of the $3,000 and found enough moonshine in the bottle to meet the same fate as the other three."

The Slaters were living in the old Borland House on the Stampede grounds at that time, so it wasn't long before Walter found the sorry group and alerted bank manager Jimmy Gould at the 150. "Rushing up as quickly as travel would permit in those days, he was lucky enough to find the money intact in old Bob's pocket."

Just prior to all this, the bank at the 150 Mile House was called the Bank of British North America. According to a formal document drawn up on September 19, 1913, the Cariboo Trading Company, which owned the 150 Mile Ranch and townsite, agreed "to lease three rooms in the old Paxton house" to the Bank of British North America for two years. The rent was set at $20 a month.

At that time the Bank of British North America was an old, established institution with branches all across Canada. The one at Richfield, for instance, was established in 1865. In 1918 it was taken over by the Bank of Montreal and the name changed, which of course included the branch at the 150 Mile House.

From gold-rush days up until 1919, the 150 Mile House had been a busy centre, but it gradually diminished in importance when Williams Lake came into being. Eventually the Bank of Montreal closed its branch at the 150, but the old house continued to be used as a bunkhouse, then a family home for many years.

It was torn down in 1952 when a new bridge was constructed across the creek, thus wiping out another bit of 150 Mile history.

The bank at the 150 Mile was the two-storey white building, centre left. In the background, centre, is the original 150 Mile stopping house and store dating back to gold-rush days. Only the big barn, right, remains today. (BCARS A-03905)

The Felker Story

Every time I drive into Williams Lake from my home at Chimney Lake, I pass lovely little Felker Lake, so named for one of the most historic families in the Cariboo. A little farther along, the road bisects the Felker Lake ranch, now owned by Geraldyne and Joe Doyle, and I try to imagine what it must have been like in 1877 when Henry Patrick Felker first began clearing the land for a homestead.

He was only seventeen years of age when he set out from his parents' home at the 144 Mile with a crew of Chinese labourers to follow the well-worn wagon track to St. Joseph's Mission. From there a narrow trail led over a ridge to the beautiful valley where Chimney Creek tied together three lakes on its meandering path to the Fraser River. The two upper ones, originally known as the Twin Lakes because they were so close together, would later be named Chimney and Felker, and the smallest was named for Charles Bronson (later spelled Brunson), who first pre-empted the land.

Although it was dense bush, Henry Patrick's land was criss-crossed with trails dating back to gold-rush days and worn smooth by natives, prospectors, and pioneer settlers. Following the Fraser River Trail, they cut off at Springhouse and headed for the Chimney/Felker area. From there, trails branched everywhere, with the main one leading over to the Onward Ranch and the 150 Mile House, an important junction on the Cariboo Wagon Road. Another snaked down the Chimney Creek valley to the mouth of the Fraser River, where a small scow ferried people across to the Chilcotin.

My story, however, starts with Henry Patrick's parents, German-born George Heinrich "Henry" Felker and his wife Antonette, who

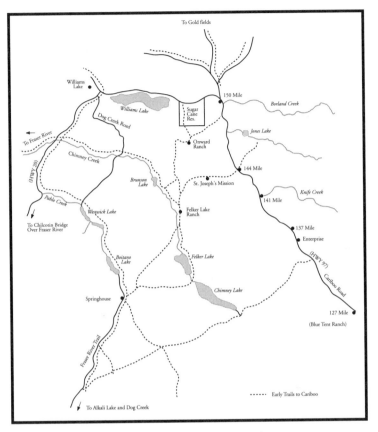

Early trails in the Chimney/Felker Lakes area.

immigrated to the U.S. in 1848 and, after a long difficult trek by wagon train from New York, finally reached the California gold fields. In 1858, when gold was found in Fraser's River, Henry hurried north and settled at Yale with his family, which now included two sons and a daughter. In 1860 their third son, Henry Patrick, later known as Harry or "H.P.," was born here. There would eventually be seven children.

By the spring of 1862 the Felkers were on the move again, this time to the Cariboo. Plodding along by horseback and covered wagon, they finally reached a spot north of Lac la Hache where they set up a temporary home and saloon in a huge blue tent. Known as the Blue Tent Ranch, it was also Mile 127 on the Cariboo Wagon

Road that was being con-
structed to the gold fields,
and the Felkers soon put up
a large log stopping house.

*Gold-rush
pioneers Henry
and Antonette
Felker.* (COURTESY
DOLLY PETROWITZ)

In 1865, through a series
of misfortunes, Henry Felker
lost his ranch and went back
to the States, but returned in
1868 and obtained land at
the 144 Mile where he built
another log roadhouse.

The youngsters rode horseback four miles
to school at St. Joseph's Mission and also
helped on the ranch; the boys—George, John
Richard, Harry, and William—with outside
chores; the girls—Joanna, Louisa, and
Emma—with cooking and cleaning. Antonette was a scrupulous
housekeeper and would fumigate a room for bedbugs, then have
Henry test it as "they would be sure to bother him." Needless to
say, the 144 Mile House became a popular stopping place for
teamsters heading for Barkerville.

Over the years Henry acquired more and more land and enlarged
his herds of cattle and horses. After his death in 1894, the oldest
son, George, stayed with the home ranch; Dick was already
established at the 118 Mile, and Will was living in a log home beside
San Jose Creek not far from the 144 Mile. (Will died of cancer at his
parents' home in 1902 when he was just 36, and his ghost reputedly
roamed the upper floor ever after.)

Harry, in the meantime, was spending those early years between
the homestead at the 144 Mile and his Chimney Creek property. He
and his brothers George and Will formed the Felker Brothers
Company around 1880 and began buying up more land around the
144 Mile and in the Chimney Creek valley. Eventually the Felker
holdings stretched all the way from Harry's original 160-acre pre-
emption to include property around Felker Lake and both ends of
Chimney Lake plus a big chunk in the middle.

Going back and forth from Chimney Creek to 144 Mile House,
Harry often stopped at the Mission to help the priests, and it was
here that he met a slim young English lass by the name of Helena
"Nellie" Richardson, who was helping to teach English and other

skills to the Indian girl students. In 1894 they were married at the Mission, and their first son, Henry George, was born the following year in their little cabin on Chimney Creek.

Soon after, H.P. built a big, eleven-room, three-storey log home, the outside covered with siding brought from the coast, then painted yellow. The walls downstairs were finished in wood tongue-and-groove panelling, while the upstairs bedrooms were papered with heavy, expensive gold-and-white oilcloth.

Henry "Harry" Patrick Felker, pioneer of the Chimney/Felker Lake area. (COURTESY DOLLY PETROWITZ)

It became a handy stopping place for travellers, and it's said that even the notorious train robber Bill Miner stopped here one day. "He just asked to buy some beef," says Harry's granddaughter Esther Wainwright. "He didn't use his real name, so they didn't realize who he was."

The 144 Mile House, built by Henry Felker Sr. in 1868, was purchased by Orville and Marie Fletcher in 1948 and is still owned by the Fletcher family. The house burned to the ground in 1964, but the old barn, granary, and blacksmith shop still remain. (COURTESY SYD WESTERN)

The Chimney Creek valley and the old Felker ranch as it looked in the 1960s. The picturesque Russell fence, a trademark of the Cariboo-Chilcotin, has since vanished and been replaced by barbed wire.

The rest of the Felker children were born in this house. One of their sons died in infancy, but the others—Henry, Peter, Tom, George (known as Bud), and Fred—all went to school at St. Joseph's Mission and remained in the Cariboo for the rest of the their lives. The girls—Josephine, Winnie, Mary, and Monica "Dolly"—were sent out to St. Ann's Academy, travelling by wagon or stagecoach to Ashcroft, then by train to New Westminster. Dolly was the only one to return to the Cariboo to stay. She married Archie Petrowitz of Springhouse in 1928, and later they took over the ranch at the southwest end of Chimney Lake, originally owned by Archie's father.

H.P. raised fine horses and cattle, and each fall he would drive his herd to Ashcroft, stopping to pick up more from the Mission and other ranchers along the way. Before leaving Ashcroft he would place Nellie's order for such staples as flour and sugar, and for boxes of dried fruit that were sent up by stage.

Henry Patrick died in 1937 at age 77. "He was still active and riding his favourite horse, Fox, until shortly before his death," says grandson Doug Petrowitz. Just a year later his log house, which had seen so much history pass its doors, burned to the ground. Nellie carried on with the ranch and built the present log home on the same site a couple of years later. When she died in 1949, the property was divided, with son Fred keeping the home ranch until his death in 1964.

My husband Clive and I drove out to Chimney Lake for the first time in 1951 to visit our good friends Nell and Sam Mitchell, who owned the Chimney Lake Lodge. We took the only route in at the time; that is, through the Sugar Cane Reserve and the Onward Ranch, then up a steep hill to the ridge behind, not realizing we were travelling an historic trail. It was a ghastly road, full of potholes and slimy with gumbo when it rained, and few people tried it in winter—or even summer, for that matter. It has now fallen into disuse and is virtually impassable. In 1959 a narrow dirt road that led in to Brunson Lake was extended to connect with the old route, thus bypassing the dreadful hill. Today it is a modern paved road that brings hundreds of summer people as well as permanent residents to the Chimney/Felker area.

Joe Doyle, present owner of the Felker ranch, stands by the second Felker ranchhouse, built around 1940.

Recently I toured the old ranch with former BC Rail coordinator Joe Doyle, who acquired the property in 1966. There is little left now to remind one of Henry Patrick's large enterprise: just a couple of small log outbuildings and his big barn, now collapsed, down by the creek where you can see traces of the original trail from Springhouse that brought so many gold seekers this way almost 140 years ago.

Chimney Creek is believed to have been named for a stone chimney near the creek's mouth at the Fraser River, all that was left in later years of a priest's cabin built at an Indian settlement there in 1842. Chimney Lake takes its name from the creek.

The Haunted House

The most enduring historical landmark in the Felker Lake area was a tall log "haunted house" that stood on the hillside between the two lakes for 112 years.

It really wasn't haunted, according to the Felker family. There were no tales of murder and buried gold, no wraith-like shapes moaning around its shad-owed walls. Somehow it just *looked* haunted, enticing youngsters to creep up to the bleak old house in the dark of a moonless night to look for spooks.

The land was pre-empted in 1881 by H.O. "Bill" Bowe of Alkali Lake and William Meason of Little Dog Creek. To "prove up" the property and get a Crown grant, Meason built the log house—probably the first home in the upper Chimney Creek valley—then did the necessary clearing, ploughing, and fencing.

With two bedrooms upstairs and a kitchen and living room downstairs, bisected by a flight of stairs, it was extremely well-built, using big, flat, hand-hewn timbers, neatly dove-tailed at the corners.

After they gained title to the land, the two partners sold the property to the Felker Brothers Company. It would remain in the Felker family for over 100 years.

The last occupants were Caroline and Bill Bellmond (his mother was Emma Felker), who lived there from 1921 to 1922. "It was a lovely comfortable home, snug and warm," Caroline told me years later. It was there that her first child, Vera, was born with the help of an Indian woman fishing nearby on Felker Lake.

For 70 years the little house sat silent, gradually deteriorating, until in 1992 Grant and Rita Corbett purchased the property. They tried to move the "haunted house" the following year, but some of the logs were rotten, and it collapsed in the attempt. And so the lonely sentinel on the hillside, a reminder of an earlier pioneer age, disappeared.

The Chinese in the Cariboo

The history of the first Chinese immigrants to British Columbia has been told many times—how they came by the hundreds from China in the 1860s, lured by tales of the "Gold Mountain." Many followed the white prospectors heading for Quesnel Forks and Barkerville, working the creeks and rivers as they went, while others laboured on the building of the Cariboo Wagon Road. In 1881 thousands more were brought in to lay track during construction of the Canadian Pacific Railway. The early Chinese arrivals were heartily disliked, not only for the colour of their skin and their foreign speech, but also because of their willingness to work for lower wages. This put many white labourers out of work.

The Chinese were a hard-working, thrifty people and sent most of their money back to family in China. Many stayed the rest of their lives in the Cariboo-Chilcotin, and almost every ranch had a Chinese man who was an integral part of the household—doing the cooking, cleaning, and gardening. The Chinese were born irrigators and the systems of ditches they built in the late 1800s on many ranches, and for mining ventures along rivers, can still be seen today.

My stories of the early Chinese in the Cariboo are tales you might not find in other history books.

Chinese in Barkerville in the Early 1900s

In 1952, Alexandria pioneer Henry Windt told the *Williams Lake Tribune* of his experiences after moving to Barkerville in 1901. He

Main street of Barkerville around 1900. (BCARS A-03791 GLENN LARIO COLLECTION)

had vivid memories of the Chinese men who lived there at the time.

There were two "tongs" or factions of Chinese in Barkerville then, far outnumbering the whites, he said. To secure men to work in the mines, owners had to see Yan War, head of one of these tongs, and make the necessary arrangements.

They dressed alike in loose coats with no lapels, loose trousers, and a black hat somewhat similar to a cowboy hat. Their main food, rice, came from China in 50-pound mats made of woven rice straws. Pork, their preferred meat, was supplied by an enterprising merchant who started out from Ashcroft to walk a herd of pigs to Barkerville. By the time he reached his destination, the pigs were well fattened up by the rich forage to be had along the way. The Chinese kept the pigs alive during the summer, then killed and froze them when winter set in.

Gambling and opium smoking were legal and widespread in those days, with the favourite game being chuck-luck. It helped them pass the long hard winter months when work in the mines came to a halt.

The Chinese had their own medicine men, who no doubt relied on herbs to a great extent. Windt recalled a time when he cut his foot badly with an axe while splitting pine trees. As the nearest doctor was miles away, he was attempting to treat the foot himself, with poor results. One day Ah Cow, the Chinese doctor, saw the wound and took matters into his own hands. Opening the wound, he shaved minute particles from a deer horn into the cut. "The foot healed perfectly and I had no more trouble," Windt remarked.

Another Chinese man by the name of "Get-um-sum" Sing supplied water to the housewives of Barkerville. The nickname was coined from his invariable reply when he was asked for water—"I get um sum." Get-um-sum dipped his water from the river in two large cans attached to a long pole balanced across his shoulders. Housewives paid ten cents a can or three dollars a month for the water, which was emptied into a whiskey barrel kept on the doorstep for this purpose.

Naming Ah Bau Creek

When the Pacific Great Eastern Railway finally reached Prince George in 1952, the ceremony to drive the last spike connecting the rails between Quesnel and Prince George took place at Ah Bau Creek, named for a Chinese placer miner who in the early 1900s lived in a small cabin high up the winding stream.

Several times a year he came out to Quesnel and mingled with white miners and freighters at the Occidental and Cariboo Hotel bars. He would lay his moose-skin poke of gold dust on the bar and offer to buy drinks on the house. He played poker until dawn, sometimes winning, more often losing, but always cheerful.

One spring Ah Bau did not appear as usual, and when police made their way to his lonely cabin, they found the old Chinese man in his rough handmade armchair where he had obviously been sitting for most of the winter. On the table near him was a teapot and two drinking bowls neatly arranged as though he was waiting for a visitor.

He was buried in his little cabbage patch with his battered gold pan bottom side up to signify the end of the day's labour.

Jack Chow and the Lakeview

One of the first businessmen in Williams Lake was Chinese hotel owner Jack Chow, who by the summer of 1920 had his Lakeview Hotel, the first to go up in the new village, ready for guests.

The name "Lakeview" seems a bit strange as it was impossible to see the lake from the site, not even from the roof, but it's said Chow wanted to perpetuate the name of the hotel in Kelowna where he had previously worked.

Disaster hit Chow within a year when his hotel burned to the ground in a fire that started in the Fraser and Mackenzie store next

Jack Chow, one of the first hotel men in Williams Lake, built his second Lakeview Hotel, above, in 1921 after fire destroyed the original one. It can still be seen behind the present Lakeview Hotel.

door and wiped out half the business district. An old-timer recalled that the cellar of the Lakeview contained dozens of bottles of "near beer," and many willing helpers rushed in to rescue the hot bottles, risking bursts of flying glass in their zeal.

Chow quickly rebuilt, putting up a much better building. By 1929 it had become too small for his flourishing business, so he moved it to the back of the lot and constructed a new concrete building in front. A *Tribune* report stated that "every room will be supplied with hot and cold water, and there will also be a speaking tube and electric bell in every room." Brass spittoons were of course a must.

Old-timers remember Chow as a "wonderfully kind man; everybody liked him." From former resident Sid Pigeon I learned that Chow was a slim, good-looking man who always dressed immaculately in a blue suit and tie, with a white napkin over his arm whenever he served drinks from his well-stocked bar.

The Lakeview was one of the most important places in Williams Lake for many years, not only as a hotel and restaurant, but also as a meeting place for many organizations. Rooms were permanently set aside for Chilcotin ranchers such as Charlie Moon and R.C. Cotton, and for Cedar Creek miner Barney Boe, as a place to stay when they came to town.

Chow sold his hotel in 1945 and moved to Vancouver. Since then it has had many owners and undergone a number of renovations, but if you take a peek down the lane beside it, you can still see the historic "annex," the second hotel built by Chow almost 80 years ago.

The Only Chinese Cowboy

"I go with Indian freight wagon. We walked and walked and camped and camped. It rained. God damn it rained. We roll in blanket at night. No tent, no can get dry."

This is the way Sin Tooie, B.C.'s only Chinese cowboy, described his first trip to the Chilcotin in 1910, when he walked from Ashcroft to Hanceville. He could not speak a word of English then.

I talked to this remarkable little 76-year-old, manager of the Williams Lake Rooms, in October 1966 when he was planning a trip back to China. "If it good, maybe I not come back. If it not good ... *pfft*, I come back," he laughed, and his black eyes crinkled with humour.

Sin Tooie.

Born in 1890, he was just twenty years of age when he left his home south of Canton and sailed for Vancouver, where he boarded the train for Ashcroft. There he found a freight wagon going his way and tagged along. "It was hard time," he recalled. "God damn it was hard." It took seventeen days to get from Ashcroft to Hanceville, trudging along the trail that swung off the Cariboo Road north of Clinton, wound over to the Fraser, then through the huge Gang Ranch until he finally reached Hanceville, where he went to work at Alex Graham's C-1 Ranch at Alexis Creek. "I cowboy, I work on irrigation ditches, I learn to cook, I mend machinery, I plough, I do any damn thing." He got $30 a month and worked ten hours a day.

Somehow he saved enough to go back to China two years later and get married. A year later he was back in the Chilcotin, again working at Graham's. A professional cowboy at the Chilco Ranch by 1930, he could rope and tie a calf with the best of them but was still "doing any damn thing," cooking for 27 men, mending mowing machinery, cutting logs, butchering beef, out looking for strays.

He was 51 years old before he gave up the rough life and moved into Williams Lake, where he became cook at the Royal Cafe, then at the Lakeview Hotel. In the meantime he had been back to China five times and fathered two sons and two daughters who never came to Canada. "No money," he shrugged, "that is all. Immigration laws very stiff."

In 1947 Sin Tooie opened his own Williams Lake Cafe on First Avenue. He told how storeowner Rod Mackenzie gave him groceries and butcher Tom Hawker gave him meat to get started. Later he added a rooming house. "I start it for Indians so they have somewhere to go."

Over the years the Chinese pioneer became an inveterate traveller, hopping a bus, plane, or train to go to Quesnel, Prince George, or Vancouver. When I talked with him in 1966 he was going back to China again to see his sixteen grandchildren and three great-grandchildren for the first time. "If I no like, I come back. One crazy man, me."

Sin Tooie did indeed come back. He blew $11,000 on his last trip to China and got as far as Hong Kong. He found "too much fighting, can't stay in God damn place." So he returned to Williams Lake without even seeing his family. "I like it better here. More friends more good." He died in Vancouver in 1973.

Death of a Pioneer

In early February 1999, Michael Feeney, 29, was sentenced to life in prison for the 1991 second-degree murder of 85-year-old Frank Boyle of Likely, who was bludgeoned to death with a crowbar in what was described as an "overkill situation."

I was shocked and saddened when I heard of the murder of Frank Boyle. Just seven years before his tragic death I talked to this kindly old pioneer, a man who had tackled many things during his lifetime and remembered them all vividly.

He was a small man, standing five foot seven inches with a slim wiry frame, but the story of his life was one of epic proportions.

He spoke casually of his three years with a National Geographic expedition in Alaska; of driving freight wagons and stagecoaches in the Cariboo; of blacksmithing at the Bullion Mine; of being a big-game guide and running a resort at Likely with his beloved wife Dolly—and of a host of other pursuits in a remarkable life that started out at Empire Valley.

His Irish grandfather was Calvin Boyle who, with his brother, trekked north through the Cariboo in 1859, heading for the Yukon. Later, Calvin retraced his steps and ended up in Empire Valley, becoming one of the first settlers in the valley.

He had one daughter and five sons. One was Frank Boyle Sr. who, as a young man, met and fell in love with Jane Salmon, whose family ranched across the Fraser River at Soda Creek. The couple were married at St. Joseph's Mission in 1899, and one of their son Frank's most prized possessions was an old Singer treadle sewing

machine that his father ordered
from Eaton's Winnipeg store in
1897 as an engagement present for
his bride-to-be.

"It came by CPR to Ashcroft,
and the BX stage brought it to Soda
Creek. Then my Dad put it on a
pack horse to take across [the
Fraser River] on the little ferry to
the Salmon Ranch."

The young couple lived in
Empire Valley at first, and that's
where Frank Jr. was born in 1906,
but when grandfather Calvin sold
the ranch in 1911, the family all
moved to Upper Hat Creek. After
serving overseas in World War I,
Frank's father returned in 1919 but

Frank Boyle in later years,
standing at the door of his
mobile home in Likely.
(COURTESY PATRICIA BARON)

died at Ashcroft two years later from shell shock.

Always deeply devoted to his mother, who had lost a leg in a
shotgun accident, Frank then moved with her to Williams Lake,
where he went to work for Harry Curtis, who operated a sawmill on
the hillside west of the little village. But in 1922, when his mother
heard of the Cedar Creek gold rush, she wanted to go, despite being
on crutches. "We drove out with a four-horse team," recalled Frank.
"Likely didn't exist then; it was known as Quesnel Dam."

They finally reached the historic old mining town of Quesnel
Forks, still home to about 60 Chinese and several white families,
and that's where Frank celebrated his sixteenth birthday. There his
mother stayed, renting a house for five dollars a month, while Frank
worked that first winter helping surveyor G.R. Bagshawe mark
mining claims at Cedar Creek. The snow was sixteen feet deep.

His next job, which lasted several years, was blacksmithing for
the gold mines—going from Kitchener to Spanish Creek, sharpening
drills and picks, straightening crowbars and shovels. Then he worked
for Bill Parker, owner of the Big Lake Ranch, who had the mail and
freight contract between Williams Lake and Keithley.

Realizing Frank was a good driver despite his size, Parker soon
had the young lad driving Concord stagecoaches and freight wagons.
Sent into Williams Lake with a long string of orders to haul out, Frank

Frank Boyle often hauled big freight outfits like this for William Parker of Big Lake, who is shown ready to leave the 59 Mile House. (BCARS A-03890)

would put the horses up at Claude Pigeon's barn overnight. "Williams Lake in those days was nothing much," he said. "Horses and cattle wandered up and down the streets." He even took part in some of the early Stampedes, "riding a couple of times in the Roman Race [standing on the backs of two horses] and doing some bronc-riding."

After picking up all the orders and mail at the Mackenzie and T.A. Moore stores, Frank would start out, taking six or seven days to make the trip back to Keithley with the loaded freight outfit sometimes pulled by a four-horse team, sometimes by six or ten. The first day he would make Crosina's 153 Mile House, next Big Lake, then Beaver Lake where there was a huge barn and kitchen facilities for drivers, then on to Morehead Lake and Quesnel Forks, and at last Keithley Creek. "That road was pretty doggone rough," Frank told me with some understatement. "We would have to stop and put rocks in the holes, and fill them with gravel and dirt. All the drivers did the same thing."

Frank also drove a team of huge Clydesdale horses to Clinton and back one winter for the Gang Ranch. "I never saw such horses," he chuckled. "They were so big I had to stand on a stool to buckle the harness."

In 1926 Frank got an unusual offer. He was asked to go on a National Geographic Society expedition to Alaska to study wildlife.

Frank Boyle and his wife Dolly.
(COURTESY PATRICIA BARON)

He never knew why he was invited. "I knew which end of a horse or a cow to put a bridle on, but that's all," he laughed. There was nothing to recommend him for such an adventure.

He settled his mother in a small home alongside the old Borland House on the Stampede grounds at Williams Lake, then as one of a six-man crew went by ship to Point Barrow, there to be met by Eskimos and dog teams for the journey inland.

It was a fascinating three-year experience, learning about birds and seals and polar bears, and learning how to speak the local language, build and live in igloos, drive dog teams, and endure blizzards. Frank found he had a natural affinity for birds and could lift wild geese off their nests while crew members counted the eggs. Others attempting it were severely bitten.

Back in the Cariboo by November 1929, Frank spoke casually of the next eighteen years, working at odd jobs around Williams Lake—four years with the PGE Railway, then in 1938 going to work for Newt Clare in his garage on Railway Avenue and becoming a licensed mechanic. He also helped Syd Western in his Oliver Theatre

Frank Boyle rode broncs and competed in the Roman Race at the Williams Lake Stampede in the late 1920s.
(COURTESY BEN CLARKE)

Likely in the 1990s.

and got his licence as a projectionist, taking time off in the fall to act as a guide for American big-game hunters in the Likely area.

Then his mother, whom he had provided for all his life, died— and his life changed radically. In 1945 he met Dolly Washbrook of Vancouver, who was working at the newly opened Famous Cafe in Williams Lake, and they were married at Likely in August 1947.

Frank's life, with Dolly as a happy companion, remained one of unusual and varying occupations in the Likely area. In 1949 they took over the job of managing the Northern Lights Lodge for owner Fred Hale, an association which lasted until 1958. Moving to the coast for a few years, the couple returned to their beloved Cariboo and opened their own restaurant, "Dolly's Cafe" at Likely, a popular enterprise that they ran until 1971.

Even after retirement the couple kept busy in community affairs and delighted in repairing toys and dolls to give at Christmas to small patients in Cariboo Memorial Hospital.

Dolly died in 1983, but Frank continued to live alone in his mobile home on Cedar Point Road, surrounded by trees and the memories of a life rich with never-to-be-forgotten experiences ... until he was found murdered there on June 8, 1991.

Note: At the time of writing, Michael Feeney is appealing his conviction.

Lord of 100 Mile House

(Based on the unfinished manuscript of the late Carol Shaw)

In the first decade of the last century, there were very few people in the 100 Mile area, and it took a titled Englishman to foresee the possibilities of future development.

He was William Cecil, the fifth Marquis of Exeter, whose title dated back some 400 years to the time when Queen Elizabeth I reigned over England, and her Lord Treasurer and trusted adviser was Lord Burghley, the first William Cecil. In 1912, after several trips to British Columbia's interior at the invitation of Major Charles G. Cowan of Kamloops, the Marquis bought 15,000 acres encompassing the 100 Mile area and known as the Bridge Creek Ranch.

Cowan managed the ranch until 1930, when the Marquis brought out his 21-year-old second son, Lord Martin Cecil, who had just completed a three-year-stint with the Royal Navy, to take over. They travelled by train to Kamloops, then by car to 100 Mile, and Martin later recalled seeing very little habitation during the long five-hour drive over the rough, twisting Cariboo Wagon Road. "I felt I was a long way from anywhere."

Finally they reached 100 Mile House, so named because it was 100 miles from Lillooet, Mile Zero on the original Cariboo Wagon Road. The population numbered about a dozen, and a little cluster of buildings, including an old stopping house, made up this "wide spot in the road." The original part of the roadhouse had been built in 1861 during gold-rush days, but it had been added on to many times, resulting in a row of dilapidated mismatched buildings, freezing cold in winter. Many of the upstairs bedrooms were windowless. "There was no heat except for a stovepipe that ran through; you could look out through the shakes," recalled Martin.

Born in 1909 in Stamford, England, he had lived most of his life in the family home called Burghley House, "built in the 1500s with 200 or 300 rooms," so his new residence must have come as somewhat of a shock.

One of the first projects the handsome young Englishman tackled was the building of the 100 Mile Lodge (behind the present Red Coach Inn), which he designed and built with the help of two or three men. "I suppose it

Lord Martin in the 1930s shortly after his arrival.

was a good thing I was quite ignorant or I wouldn't have gone ahead," he mused. "I had no prior experience."

He sat up late at night in his tiny room in the old stopping house, reading books on construction methods by the light of an oil lamp, and soon, with rough uneven lumber obtained at a small sawmill on Bridge Creek, the project was underway. He even devised a plumbing system, building a flume to bring water from Bridge Creek, then pumping it up to a thousand-gallon water tank he built above his new lodge. This system

The original 100 Mile stopping house, where Lord Martin first lived. (BCARS A-03897)

only worked until freeze-up, of course, at which time they would go back to outhouses and hauling water from the creek. But the part-time amenity, along with the 32-volt electric system he installed, made the 100 Mile Lodge one of the most "modern" stopping houses on the road. It was certainly a tremendous improvement on the old bug-infested roadhouse, which burned to the ground in 1937 "with a terrible loss of life, none of it human," observed Lord Martin.

As a working cowboy/rancher, Lord Martin soon adopted the casual style of the Cariboo.

Gradually the man who had been educated to be a gentleman became a "jack of all trades" and adopted the casual shirt, jeans, and cowboy hat so practical for a working rancher in the Cariboo. He found it an easy transition, even though social life in the Cariboo was a far cry from the grand balls in England.

Martin tried to introduce polo to the Cariboo, rounding up the B.C. policeman stationed at Clinton, the storekeeper, and various cowboys for games held on a rough pasture. He also built a golf course, but nobody was very interested except the few sheep that liked to bed down on the greens. He was game to try local sports, however, and fashioned himself a pair of skis out of birch boards held on by thongs, but he didn't get a good bend on the front parts so they dug into the snow. His foray into that sport was short-lived.

As well as running the huge family ranch, Martin also took over management of the Highland Ranch owned by Lord Egerton of Tatton, making a total of 50,000 acres. But he had good men like Alex Morrison at 100 Mile and Don Laidlaw at 105 Mile to help him, as well as many Indians. "They were good workers, knew the country, hours meant nothing to them, and together we got along very well," his Lordship recalled.

Those were the years of the great depression, when "it was impossible to get more than five dollars for a cow." On the two great ranches there were 2,000 head of cattle and 2,000 sheep, "and you couldn't sell them." Instead his Lordship worked deals by trading sheep for hay, and he finally got rid of them altogether. "Ranching never was a really profitable business," he would later remark philosophically, "but there's something basic about it that permits survival under very adverse conditions."

Cattlemen by this time were realizing they needed to organize themselves if they were to survive, and the young neophyte at 100 Mile was soon actively involved. Up to this time, competitive bidding for cattle was unheard of, and ranchers had to accept prices named by the buyers of two big meat-packing companies, Swifts and Burns, who toured the country, sometimes offering no more than 1-1/2 cents per pound.

The first effort to change the system came in 1934 when R.C. Cotton of Riske Creek formed the Cariboo Stockmen's Association, with Lord Martin as vice-president. In 1935 Martin worked on a committee headed by George Mayfield, which came up with the bold idea of a co-operative marketing scheme: cattle would be brought to the Williams Lake stockyards and sold at auction. That led to the formation of the Cariboo Cattlemen's Association in 1943, with Martin as its first president, a position he held until 1954. He was later president of both the provincial and national cattlemen's organizations.

During this time Martin was running his ranch, keeping an eye on the lodge and general store, and getting up in the night to fix the water or power systems if needed. He was the postmaster for many years, served as Imperial Oil agent, and built the first school in the community.

He was also searching for his spiritual identity, and he found it in 1940 in the writings of Lloyd Arthur Meeker, an American visionary who had incorporated his teachings into a program called the Emissaries of Divine Light, with headquarters in Loveland, Colorado. After a number of trips to Loveland, where he became deeply committed to his new faith, Lord Martin started a small group at 100 Mile House in 1948. It became the Canadian Emissary headquarters, and when Meeker was killed in a plane crash in 1954, Martin assumed the leadership of what would become an international movement numbering thousands of people. Basically a very shy man, he became an excellent speaker and travelled all over the world. He also authored several books.

During the 1950s and 60s, lumbering transformed sleepy 100 Mile House into the fastest growing village in British Columbia, and

The main street of 100 Mile House as it looked in the 1940s.

the beginnings of a modern-day town began to sprout on Lord Martin's best hayfields. He initially leased the land, which was known as Bridge Creek Estates, but when the village was incorporated in 1965, the properties were offered for sale. Ross Marks, who had arrived in 1948 to become Martin's trusted friend and manager, was the first mayor, a position he held for 21 years.

By this time Martin's 100 Mile Lodge had become increasingly inadequate, so under his direction a new development was planned— this was the building of the Red Coach Inn motel complex, which fronted on the highway near where the original stopping house had stood. Opened in 1966, it is a lovely warm hostelry, famous for its dining facilities and gift shop. Standing beside it is a handsome BX stagecoach that once plied the Cariboo Wagon Road, one of the few still in existence today.

The old Lodge then became a combination community kitchen/ business centre, and the old log blacksmith and carpentry shop behind it, built at the turn of the century, was beautifully restored as a chapel.

In 1981, with the death of his elder brother David, Lord Martin succeeded to the title of Seventh Marquis of Exeter and the following year travelled to Westminster to take his seat in the House of Lords.

But home was still 100 Mile House in the Cariboo, and here he lived unless he was travelling to far-flung places in his role as Emissary leader or to England in connection with his parliamentary duties. In 1980 he was the recipient of the first "Pioneer of the Year" award given by the 100 Mile House & District Historical Society.

The 100 Mile Lodge, built by Lord Martin in the 1930s from construction manuals he studied by the light of a coal-oil lamp.

Death came to Lord Martin Cecil, often termed "the founding father" of 100 Mile House, on January 12, 1988, in Royal Inland Hospital at Kamloops. He was 77. His ashes were interred in a newly created private cemetery behind the old Lodge. Before his death he predicted changes within the ministry, and this has certainly come to pass with a significant drop in the number of Emissary adherents worldwide. Undoubtedly the loss of their strong, dynamic leader, along with changes in today's spiritual beliefs, contributed to the decline.

Lord Martin came as a stranger with little knowledge of the region or its customs. He left having made 100 Mile House a better place. He helped to establish new businesses and ensured the orderly growth of the bustling village; donated Centennial Park, where the remains of the little sawmill that produced the rough-hewn boards for his Lodge can still be seen; and left a legacy of kindness, hard work, and a new perspective of religion.

Many of his family, including his second wife Lillian, daughter Marina, and three of his four grandchildren, still live in the 100 Mile House area. His son Michael, the current Marquis of Exeter, lives in Oregon.

(All uncredited photos courtesy of Lillian Cecil).

Travelling the Great North Road

"Travel the Great North Road and Alaska Highway through Romantic Cariboo," burbled the government brochure published in the 1930s extolling the wonders to be seen through B.C.'s interior.

It was not referring to the Alaska Highway as we know it today—the road pushed north from Dawson Creek as a war measures act in 1942—but a completely different proposal that would have seen construction start at Hazelton, *west* of Prince George.

This was part of an international venture designed to knit together Mexico, the United States, and Canada through the Yukon to Alaska with thousands of miles of new highway construction.

The route in B.C. was promoted as the Great North Road. Starting at Vancouver, it ambled through the Fraser Valley, climbed the jagged walls of the Fraser Canyon, and turned north at Cache Creek to follow the Cariboo Highway to Prince George and over to Hazelton where the proposed Alaska Highway would start. But for some reason it never lived up to the grandiose dream.

The brochure makes it all sound so wonderful, but I can't help doubting some of the hyperbole. For instance, the Cariboo Highway is touted as "safe, smooth and spectacular—the most glorious highway in the world."

In the 1930s? They had to be kidding.

You only have to read the account of a chap with the initials H.B.W., who with a nameless companion started out from Prince George in a little Ford flivver to try and catch the train at Ashcroft, a trip that took them ten hours during the first blizzard of 1933. His wonderfully descriptive narrative, full of humour and vivid imagery,

A flivver on a section of the Great North Road (now Highway #1) east of Yale in the 1920s or 30s. (BCARS C-01325)

appeared in the *Victoria Times* that year and certainly gives a different impression of the Great North Road:

> We came to know a lot of things about the Great North Road that we never suspected. Under the snow, the Road is a treacherous jade who lies in wait for innocents like us, who lures us on and dumps us into the Fraser if she can.
>
> We slither from side to side, the steering wheel spinning. Twice we can't make the curves at all, and as we jam on our brakes we slide out to the rim of the river and our front wheels stop just two inches from the void.
>
> It is wild work and there are 300 miles ahead. Yet somehow you never think of distances up here, where men live far apart, and it never occurs to us that it is stark madness to dare the Great North Road on a day like this.
>
> At Quesnel there is always comfort to be found in Louis LeBourdais' telegraph office. Louis, that friend of everybody on the Great North Road, talks to Ashcroft and Ashcroft says there is snow there. So we are off again.
>
> Then somehow we do an incredible thing. We miss the Great North Road altogether. How, we shall never know, but in ten minutes we are utterly lost; lost on a side road that seems to lead straight into the mountains south of Barkerville.

> There is no place to turn, so we keep on ... until
> finally on a track not six feet wide and in blinding
> snow, we come to a cabin in the woods, one of those
> pathetic shanties where the braver souls of the
> depression are toughing it out on moose meat and
> potatoes.

The woman at the cabin, who was obviously from the city and
not hardened to this grim life, directs them to a shortcut back to
the highway.

> We roll and slither and heave across furrows nearly
> two feet deep. Nothing but a stout little flivver could
> bring us through alive. It roars and groans and leaps
> ahead like a drunken kangaroo, bogs down and then
> climbs out again.

Finally they are back on the main road.

> The snow is deeper now, close to a foot of it. At
> the 150 Mile a red-cheeked fellow at the gas pumps
> says we shall be lucky to reach Ashcroft in nine hours.
> He warns us gloomily against venturing further into
> the gathering dark, but crying "Excelsior" we slither
> onwards, down that white, thick, endless sheet that is
> the Great North Road.

"At the Hundred Mile House there is a roaring grate fire, and
Marie Lloyd, the hostess, looks at us with the pitying glance of a
person who would like to stop two lunatics from certain destruction."
Despite the attraction of the 50-cent meal "with all the steak you
can eat," the two travellers decide to push on.

> At night the Road changes again. In the headlights
> the snow looks dirty and strangely wrinkled and the
> wheel tracks are two black shadows.

They stop to help an inexperienced traveller who has no chains.
"We ram him hard from the rear, we push him, slithering from side
to side up the Hundred Mile Hill. We waste a precious half-hour; we
all but wreck our poor flivver.

> The snow is thicker up here on the heights, but
> there are cars ahead. We stick to the ruts, a foot and a
> half deep, and we climb up to forty miles an hour, a
> crazy speed. Let the front wheel just touch the side of
> the rut and we are spun out in a dizzy arc and zig-zag
> back and forth drunkenly before we get into the tracks
> again.

They dash through Clinton, terrifying the herds of white-faced cattle that stand stupidly by the road, and now have 55 minutes to catch the train at Ashcroft.

> Finally we see the lights of Ashcroft down in the valley, but we can't find the CPR station. We dash around in circles and finally into Ashcroft where a woman of dull wit offers to direct us—and takes us down a side road into somebody's woodshed.
>
> We circle the bare range and find the station for ourselves, where the station agent informs us, without a trace of emotion, that the train had gone through an hour ago.
>
> We had been given the wrong time.

Mind you, this all happened in the wintertime, but even by September 1949, when my husband and I first travelled from New Westminster to Williams Lake, the trip still took a good twelve to thirteen hours. From Cache Creek, the Cariboo Highway (no mention of it being the Great North Road then) was a two-lane track of rough gravel. At 83 Mile, I remember, we were delighted to hit pavement, but it only lasted to 100 Mile and then we dropped off into gravel again. The final 60-odd miles to Williams Lake seemed to take forever as we bashed and twisted our way up hill and down dale through choking dust and flying rocks.

Pavement didn't reach Williams Lake until 1955.

There is no doubt that the 1930s brochure on the Great North Road did a lot to promote the Cariboo, with wonderful descriptions of its storied past, its scenic beauties, and the delights to be had at its stopping houses and lodges, but somehow it's not surprising that the name did not endure.

Hub of the Cariboo: 140 Years of Williams Lake History

1860-1919: In gold-rush days

The first Williams Lake settlement came into being in 1860 during gold-rush days in the area now known as the Comer, about three miles from the present downtown core. That's when Philip H. Nind, the first gold commissioner, decided to make his headquarters at Williams Lake near the Indian settlement and church. Soon a couple of stopping houses, a courthouse, and a jail had been built and Williams Lake seemed destined to become a thriving city.

But in 1863, when the Cariboo Wagon Road was built to give access to the fabulous gold fields, the contractor routed it from the 150 Mile House over to Soda Creek, thus bypassing Williams Lake, and the little community eventually died.

William Pinchbeck, who had arrived with Nind in 1860 and become first constable, decided to stay, and in partnership with William Lyne he built up a magnificent farm, one of the finest in British Columbia. They grew prize wheat; built a flour mill, sawmill, distillery, and brewery; and sent their pack trains laden with bacon, ham, whisky, and produce to the flourishing gold camps.

In the meantime the Williams Lake Indian Band was gradually forced farther and farther away. Finally the band found a permanent home when the Sugar Cane Reserve was established at the head of the lake in 1884.

There were two main residences on the Pinchbeck/Lyne ranch: the Upper House in the Comer area, and the Lake House built on the present Stampede grounds in 1883. Five years later Pinchbeck bought out Lyne and took over the whole enterprise. He died in

William Pinchbeck's Lake House, later known as the Borland House, on what is now the Stampede grounds. It was dismantled around 1935.

1893 and is buried in a white picket fenced plot overlooking the lake and his old homesite.

The ranch was then purchased by Robert Borland, a pioneer packer and trader, who in turn sold it in 1912 to the Pacific Great Eastern Railway.

1919-1929: Coming of the railway

It was the coming of the Pacific Great Eastern in 1919 that brought about the birth of the city of Williams Lake as we know it today. The next ten years would see the little village of tarpaper shacks and rough frame buildings gradually overcome some of the difficulties of "growing up."

It was a time of excitement, of hard work and hard play as the early settlers built a community out of the raw land. It was an era of "firsts"—the first hotels, banks, stores, school, and church; the first

The corner of Oliver Street and Railway (Mackenzie) Avenue in the early 1920s.
(BCARS E-01433)

newspaper; the first hospital—all those things that are necessary and vital to a growing settlement.

It was an era when everyone helped everyone else, whether it was repairing a fence, building a school, or getting together to plan the first Stampedes.

But it was a growth without direction.

Although ranchers could now ship their cattle from railhead at Williams Lake instead of trail-driving their herds to Ashcroft, there seemed little else to justify the existence of the tiny cowtown.

But the decade ended on a positive note. In 1929 Williams Lake was incorporated as a village. This time it was here to stay.

1929-1939: The Dirty Thirties

This was a quiet era as the great depression settled over the land.

In Williams Lake it meant prices as low as one to two cents a pound for choice heifers and steers. It meant the setting up of relief camps.

But it also meant slow and steady growth as the first village commissioners set about building a solid foundation for the new town.

This era saw the building of wooden sidewalks, the establishment of the first airport and first air service, and the formation of a fire brigade.

Although it was still a dusty village with cows and bulls wandering the streets, there was a spirit of enthusiasm in the closely knit community, whether it was staging amateur theatricals and raising money for the hospital, sailing and ice-boating on the lake, playing hockey on the outdoor rink, or making music in the newly formed town band.

A Stampede parade winds its way down Oliver Street in the 1930s. (DODWELL STUDIO PHOTO)

Everybody attended the Stampede, which was still just a happy get-together for town and district residents with amateur cowboys throughout the Cariboo vying for purses.

War came at the end of this era, and as they did everywhere else, men rushed to join the services.

1939-1949: The war years and after

With gasoline rationing and shortages of various kinds, things were tough for the people of the Cariboo during the war years, as for the rest of the country.

Several firms had to close their doors, and the War Memorial Hospital was shut down for a time "for not having the services of an acceptable doctor."

Even the Stampede was suspended and not revived until 1947.

Railway Avenue as it looked in the 1940s.

But the little community threw itself wholeheartedly into the war effort, sparked by the Comfort Club, a little group of women who organized and staged dances, variety shows, and other community events to raise money for the parcels and regular newsletters that were sent to the local boys overseas.

With the cessation of hostilities in 1945, the little village stirred to life once more. Although beset by continuing problems with the PGE over the water system, and with Columbia Power over the diesels supplying power, the town gradually grew. Considering the population was still only 1,180 in 1949, it was quite incredible.

The first fire hall, combined with a village office, was built; 24-hour telephone and telegraph service was established; a big Elks Hall was built, burned down, and rebuilt; the massive War Memorial Arena project began; and Oliver Street and Railway Avenue were the first streets in the village to be paved.

The decade was ushered out with the cattlemen recording a bumper year, and with the establishment of a new but minor industry—lumbering.

1949-1959: Drastic changes to dusty cowtown

Residents were still using wooden sidewalks, streetlights could be counted on one hand, and "crank" telephones were still in vogue in the early 1950s, but drastic changes were in the offing.

Williams Lake still held the record for being the largest single cattle-shipping centre in the province, but lumbering soon became the major industry. And with lumbering came people—and then more and more people to run the supporting businesses and services, the new stores, modern garages, motels, and restaurants.

It was a time of fabulous growth and another era of "firsts" for the dusty cow-town. The first con-crete sidewalks and first parking meters made their appear-ance as well as the first dormitory, curl-ing rink, health unit, village hall, library, chain store, and dozens of organizations.

In 1948 Lignum Ltd. established the first planer mill in Williams Lake across from the cemetery.

Sleek new Budd cars replaced the old PGE steam engines, a new airport was constructed seven miles from town, and the old airport was turned into a new subdivision for the growing village.

This decade saw major changes in highways too. Not only was Highway 97 paved from 150 Mile into Williams Lake, but instead of going down Oliver Street and then along the river route to Soda Creek, it was now routed to by-pass the town at the "Y." Bella Coola and Chilcotin residents punched through a road link—Highway 20—to the coast.

The last of the big trail drives wended its way into Williams Lake from the Chilcotin. On the lighter side, the biggest single event was undoubtedly Princess Margaret's visit in 1958 to mark British Columbia's Centennial.

1959-1969: Williams Lake becomes a town

In this decade, man walked on the moon.

In Williams Lake we got television, our first radio station, dial phones, and our first traffic light. We also had enough population to officially become a town in 1965.

The outdoor sale ring in the 1950s at Williams Lake when it was the biggest single cattle-shipping centre in B.C. (BLACKWELL STUDIO PHOTO)

There was a great building boom in the mid-sixties, with new banks, new churches, supermarkets, and apartment blocks going up, as well as schools like Columneetza Senior High and the magnificent new Cariboo Memorial Hospital in 1962.

The old hospital was torn down except for the maternity wing, which became the town hall. By 1968 it was totally inadequate.

The first senior citizens' home was built, and the old golf course became Boitanio Park when a new course was opened up on the west ridge overlooking the town and lake. And we now had direct flights to Vancouver.

Great things were happening industrially, too. Merrill Wagner opened its big veneer plant, Gibraltar its huge copper mine at McLeese Lake, and Williams Lake was chosen as headquarters for the Cariboo Forest District. The most memorable year had to be 1967, Canada's Centennial year, and Williams Lake went all out in a wild, wonderful party that lasted for months. There were Centennial teas, fashion shows, parties, and dances, as well as beards and Centennial costumes of every description. Highlight was the marvellous gold-rush musical *The Road Runs North*, which played to packed houses at Stampede time.

All in all, a fantastic decade.

1969-1981: We're a city

The growth of Williams Lake during the 1970s was fantastic.

New subdivisions sprang into being, homes mushroomed up the hillsides, and handsome buildings started to dominate the skyline.

Looking up Oliver Street in the 1960s after Williams Lake became a town. (COURTESY *WILLIAMS LAKE TRIBUNE*)

Mini-malls replaced the old homes that once lined the downtown streets; the big new provincial building was opened; and Boitanio Mall, Williams Lake's first big shopping mall was constructed.

Two of the highlights of this era were the 1971 visit of Queen Elizabeth and Prince Philip and the 1979 Jubilee celebrations marking 50 years since Williams Lake's incorporation as a village.

Like the rest of the country, Williams Lake was hit by the recession in the 80s. But although cattle prices were down and ranchers were hit by rising prices, the lumber mills and Gibraltar's copper mine continued to operate on a reduced scale so the local economy was not as severely depressed as in some other parts of Canada.

The biggest event in this period, of course, was the inclusion of the Glendale area in the town, which in turn led to Williams Lake becoming a city on September 18, 1981.

1981-1999: Into the new millennium

There was good news and bad. In the 1980s a brand new city hall finally became a reality, as well as the Cariboo Memorial twin-arena complex, which included the Sam Ketcham pool.

But the 1990s ushered in a downturn as all of B.C. gradually sank into a recession. The final blow to Williams Lake came in 1998 when Gibralter's big copper mine at McLeese Lake was closed due to low prices.

On the upside, NW Energy Corporation's power-generating plant, which converts waste wood into electricity and is the only plant of its kind in North America, opened in 1993, and although the lumber industry was hit hard, the major mills in Williams Lake never shut down. By shifting gears to "high tech" and turning to value-added

The handsome Law Courts building was part of Williams Lake's fantastic growth between 1969 and 1981.

wood products, they continued to be the backbone of the local economy.

And despite spiralling costs and a plummeting market, ranchers still continued to bring their cattle into the Williams Lake stockyards as they had since 1920. By 1998 they were trucking them to handsome new stockyards built west of the city, where beef can now be — incredibly — bought and sold electronically, via computer.

In 1997 there was another plus with the opening of the Mount Polley gold and copper mine near Likely. In 1999 we got our first "superstore," the South Lakeside area became part of the city, and the population was tagged at close to 12,000, a figure that can be almost doubled if people in the outlying areas are included.

As Williams Lake moves into the new millennium, there is cautious optimism for an upturn in the economy, particularly with the news of the possible reopening of the Gibraltar mine in 2000.

What Should We Do With the Corpse?

Writing about the Williams Lake cemetery is a bit macabre perhaps, but also downright fascinating and at times funny.

Believe it or not, the village acquired the land for the cemetery in 1923 by sending a telegram to Premier John Oliver stating: "We are expecting a man to die in a few days and wonder what we should do with the corpse?"

The village fathers were obviously having trouble getting the Pacific Great Eastern Railway, which owned all the land around Williams Lake, to part with a chunk for a much-needed cemetery for the new town established just four years previously.

The plaintive telegram from Williams Lake made the rounds of the legislative assembly and was picked up by Vancouver daily papers—much to the embarrassment, I'm sure, of the premier and his party. The story from the *Tribune* files ends with this succinct remark: "Williams Lake got its cemetery."

But what happened to Williams Lake residents who died between 1919 and 1923?

Some were buried at St. Joseph's Mission cemetery, south of Williams Lake, including "Maida, 1886-1921, beloved wife of Francis Vere Agnew, Williams Lake's first doctor," as well as Johnny Salmon and Bernard Weetman, the two young men who died in the big fire of 1921 that levelled half of the business district.

Then there was John "Jack" Aitchison who, probably because of his unsavoury death, could not be interred in the small mission cemetery maintained by the Oblate Fathers. He was killed in a shooting affray in a cabin on First Avenue in September 1921 and

St. Joseph's Mission and Residential School in the 1920s. The cemetery, where many Cariboo pioneers are buried, is in the right foreground.

is buried alongside pioneer William Pinchbeck overlooking the Stampede grounds, right in the heart of Williams Lake. Although his remains are still there, all traces of his grave have disappeared.

One of the first graves dug in the Williams Lake cemetery was for Bernard Dugan of Dugan Lake, who was shot by a neighbour's hired man before breakfast "on a bright May morning in 1923 in a dispute over a breachy cow."

There are other equally colourful "inhabitants," such as Helen Healy Luggen, the famous British wartime spy who died of cancer at age 58 in the War Memorial Hospital at Williams Lake. A faded 1937 newspaper clipping is the only clue to her life and career:

> Mrs. Luggen, resident of Sheep Creek and housekeeper for Harry Hooper, prospector...was of high American birth. She spent 20 years in China with her first husband, Captain Timothy Healy, who was commissioner agent for a large British fur trading firm. The captain was killed in the first battle of the Great War in 1914.
>
> Directly after this catastrophe, Mrs. Luggen took up secret service work for the British government in Asia and Europe. In 1916 she was smuggled out of Germany battle-scarred, a patriot. In 1917 she was spirited across the Russian border in a laundry basket belonging to the czar's palace. She married her second husband in 1922 in Vancouver, arrived in Williams Lake five years ago.

The story leaves a lot of questions unanswered. What happened to her second husband? Why did she come to the Cariboo? Did she

The fenced graves of pioneer William Pinchbeck, right, and Jack Aitchison overlooking the Stampede grounds, as they looked in the 1920s. Today only the Pinchbeck gravesite remains. (COURTESY BEN CLARKE)

have family? Do they know she is buried at Williams Lake? Although Mrs. Luggen's grave is registered at City Hall with the site, row, and number of her grave, I could find no marker, nothing to mark her last resting place. It seems rather sad that such a courageous lady should lie unknown and unclaimed so far from the country she served so well.

The tombstone of a famous cowboy in the Williams Lake cemetery.

A touching plaque marks the grave of Lloyd "Cyclone" Smith, the only man to lose his life at a Williams Lake Stampede. It happened in 1932 when the champion bronc-rider rushed at full gallop to head off a riderless bronc. The two collided. Cyclone was crushed under his horse and died 36 hours later.

Another Stampede notable buried here is Olive (Curtis) Matheson (1908-1984), who was the first of only two women to ever compete in the dangerous Mountain Race, which saw riders hurtling down a narrow trail high on Fox Mountain to finish at the Stampede grounds.

Then there's Marcus Wayne Huston (1867-1956), a teamster who drove BX stagecoaches for many years on the Cariboo Wagon Road. Another is Arthur Haddock (1878-1961), who drove stages in

The 1932 cowboy cortege for Cyclone Smith winds its way down First Avenue past the Bank of Commerce and Maple Leaf Hotel, right, on its way to the cemetery. (COURTESY BUTCH RIFE)

the Cariboo, the Klondike, and the Nevada gold fields. In an exciting climax to his career, at age 67 he drove an old BX stagecoach at the head of an Ottawa parade celebrating the post office's mail-carrying history.

The graves of many other hardy Williams Lake people who endured primitive conditions to build the new town dot the green lawn: the Bob Blairs, the Charles Moxons, and John Dexter Smedley, the village's first chairman, who was also an accomplished architect and designed St. Peter's Anglican Church.

The first Chinese person to be buried in the local cemetery was Ah Dack, manager of the Song Lee store on Railway/Mackenzie Avenue for many years. He died in September 1932. Nearby is the grave of Wong Wah Kuey (or Wong Kuey Kim as we knew him), the last Chinese resident of Quesnel Forks, who was found frozen to death near his cabin in 1954.

A walk through a cemetery is like a walk back in time.

On a Wing and a Prayer

Bill MacKenzie of Miocene was just seventeen years of age when he made his first flight in an airplane. That was in September 1927 when he went up in the first wheeled aircraft to land at Williams Lake.

"I was so scared I think I left my fingerprints on it permanently," he later declared with a grin. The plane, called *Northern Light*, was on a mail run to the Yukon, and en route the two-man crew was "barnstorming"—that is, stopping at small villages to give citizens a chance to take a short flight and, at the same time, contribute money for the aviators' expenses.

"We paid $7 for three minutes," recalled Bill. "It was an open cockpit with just room for the pilot at back, and two passengers in front. We were not tied in, and he even did a sideways loop." No wonder Bill was frightened.

Preparations for the historic visit were made by twenty-year-old Keith Caverly, who had a garage and electrical business in Williams Lake and had also built Williams Lake's first radio station, reputedly with parts from discarded alarm clocks, defunct railway engines, and old cars. Keith piled white lime inside old truck tires to mark the boundaries for a landing strip on a former horse pasture north of the village, and lit a pile of green boughs so the billowing smoke would indicate wind direction.

(Incidentally, the old pasture had been a famous racetrack in the 1860s. Located near the first Williams Lake settlement and William Pinchbeck's stopping house and bar, it attracted people from all over the interior as well as the best horses and jockeys in the country.)

The first plane to land at Williams Lake was Northern Light, *which touched down in September 1927 on a pasture north of the village.* (COURTESY BEN CLARKE)

There was great excitement in Williams Lake on that windy Sunday just before noon when *Northern Light* touched down to a field full of spectators. Caverly, along with schoolteacher Annie Demmery, were the first couple to try their wings, followed by police sergeant Frank Gallagher. Flights continued all afternoon and the next day, and when *Northern Light* finally left, Gallagher grabbed the chance for a final quick hop to Quesnel, where he had police business.

There wasn't much air activity around Williams Lake after that, although well-known bush pilots Ginger Coote and Russ Baker were making flights in and out by float plane. But when the village of Williams Lake was incorporated in 1929, first chairman John D. Smedley immediately began agitating to acquire the land for an airport. "You're nuts," objected commissioner Syd Western. After all, an airport did seem a tad ambitious for a tiny village of 300 souls with no paved streets or streetlights.

By January 1931 the Board of Trade had managed to get the Pacific Great Eastern Railway, which owned the 80-acre chunk of land, to tentatively agree to sell the old racetrack to the village for an airport for $800. It wasn't until 1934 that Williams Lake was finally granted a temporary airport licence from the federal government—subject to the pasture being properly marked and a windsock being erected.

The following year Grant McConachie, along with Coote and Baker, inaugurated the Yukon-Southern line and began operating

The famous Williams Lake Rube Band and hundreds of people turned out to welcome Canadian Pacific Airlines in 1950 when it expanded its service to include Williams Lake. (COURTESY WILLIAMS LAKE TRIBUNE)

tri-weekly flights from Vancouver to Williams Lake, Prince George, and Edmonton and back. Airfare from Vancouver to Williams Lake was $35 return.

Keith Caverly became airport manager, but he and other volunteers like Tony Woodland and Bert Levens never got paid for their work; they did it for the love of it. They built a little shed that served as the first "terminal," and with the help of the Public Works bulldozer, maintained the field. From their home, which bristled with towers, Keith and his wife Irene operated their radio station 24 hours a day, guiding pilots into the tiny airport where cows often had to be shooed away so planes could land.

Even though administration of the Williams Lake airport was eventually taken over by the federal Department of Transport, troubles plagued it for some years, and both airmail and passenger service would be suspended from time to time—usually because the runway was too short.

The runway was still unpaved and the terminal a small nondescript building when my husband Clive and I took over the *Williams Lake Tribune* in 1950. It was the same year that Canadian Pacific Airlines expanded its northern service to include Williams Lake, and we naturally covered the big event along with about 500

The first air show in 1958 at the first Williams Lake airport, which is now a subdivision. (COURTESY WILLIAMS LAKE TRIBUNE)

enthusiastic people (half the town) who deserted the village to welcome the plane and airline officials on its inaugural flight.

"I've never seen anything like it for a town this size," said big Grant McConachie, CPA president, as the visitors were engulfed by the friendly mob.

The hit of the day was Williams Lake's Rube Band headed by Bill Sharpe. Arriving in an old stagecoach, the band members kept everybody entertained with their music and antics, and visitors gleefully took turns riding in the coach.

Dozens of horsemen, headed by Ted Plante, mingled with the crowd, and one of the stewardesses in her blue uniform and red kerchief joined in the informal fun by borrowing a horse for a smart gallop to the end of the runway. Did the ghosts of those jockeys of long ago watch in amazement, I wonder?

The still-unpaved runway could only handle DC-3s when the move was made to a new airport, seven miles north on Highway 97, in 1960. The old airport was soon developed as a new subdivision and designated Ninth and Tenth Avenues, but even today it is often referred to as the "airport subdivision."

Williams Lake's airport, with its modern terminal and three daily flights to and from Vancouver, has come a long way since that day in 1927 when Bill MacKenzie made his first flight in *Northern Light* and left his fingerprints embedded on the edge of the cockpit.

The story of *Northern Light* ends on a sad note. Two winters later the little plane crashed through the ice on the Yukon River, killing the pilot.

The Polar Bear Scheme

One of the most ambitious army training exercises ever attempted in Canada during World War II took place in the Cariboo-Chilcotin.

Called the Polar Bear Expedition, it tested the endurance of men and machinery in a massive two-month winter exercise starting at Williams Lake and winding across the harsh, wind-swept Chilcotin plateau and through snow-covered coastal mountains to Bella Coola.

I first learned of the Expedition from David Irvine of North Vancouver, who was with the Royal Canadian Ordinance Corps and one of 1,000 men involved in the huge scheme.

"We formed up in Prince George around December 1944," Irvine wrote. "A number of army units were involved including Signals and Engineers, as well as ski troops, pack horse troops, artillery, infantry, and Canadian, British, and American observers. I was with the advance party that set up the Spare Parts Section for the base camp at Williams Lake in January 1945. We had to clean out a stock barn and set up bins for the parts. It was really cold, and we were housed in big twelve-man tents heated with drum stoves—which were usually out—set up at the stockyards on wood platforms."

The late Alex Fraser, former minister of highways, was also among those stationed at Williams Lake. As a member of the Royal Canadian Army Service Corps, he too remembered being billeted in the tents when the temperature dropped to 30 below zero "and all we had for heat were pot-bellied stoves with green wood that would not burn."

Big twelve-person tents at the Williams Lake stockyards housed
servicemen involved in the 1945 Polar Bear Expedition.
(COURTESY COLIN MACDONALD)

Hundreds of men and tremendous amounts of equipment were amassed at Williams Lake. "The men had never heard of or seen some of the equipment," wrote Irvine. There were snowmobiles like small tanks, two-man motor toboggans, and different types of small tractors that he described as M27s, M29s, and Weasels.

D-Day for the exercise was February 15, when the force moved westward to the Fraser Canyon, crossing on the old Sheep Creek suspension bridge that groaned and creaked and swayed with the weight of men and vehicles.

Enduring temperatures that ranged from 30 below zero to 55 above, and confronting snowbanks fifteen feet deep, the troops day by day pushed through the bleak countryside. A main supply point was established at Bull Canyon near Alexis Creek, a second one at Kleena Kleene, and an emergency landing strip made on One-Eye Lake. Then it was on to Anahim Lake, 235 miles from Williams Lake, where another supply point was built and an airstrip laid out on the lake.

"During the exercise," reported one Vancouver daily, "the men destroyed 'enemy' positions and routed four black bears who left the area after being disturbed from their hibernation by the firing."

The cowboy spirit of the Cariboo-Chilcotin must have infected the troops as "the monotony of the trail life was broken several times when the pack train troops staged impromptu rodeos when new horses had to be broken."

The 128-horse pack train transported heavy howitzers by devising a form of Indian travois. (COURTESY FRED LONG)

According to the newspaper, the pack train was unique. "In addition to packing in all sorts of essential supplies, the 128-horse pack train provided transport for 75 mm mountain howitzers, which they accomplished by taking a lesson from Indians and building 'travois'—two poles lashed together and trailed behind the pack horse over the long snow trails."

Ron Campbell is another man who has vivid memories of the Polar Bear Expedition. Stationed with the army at Chilliwack and a packer since the age of thirteen, he was a natural to head the #1 Royal Canadian Pack Transport Troop, a singular branch of the Canadian army.

Interviewed by the *Nechako Independent* in 1991, he told of the shipment of rum that arrived at Williams Lake destined for Bella Coola. Hauled to Anahim Lake by truck, it was then taken over by Ron's packers for the trip down into the valley.

However, his enterprising men found "they could carefully break the neck off a bottle, drink most of the rum, pour some into the box to make it look like it had broken in transit, then replace the bottle, neck and all."

But it was not all fun and games on the rigorous journey across the Chilcotin plateau in winter. As well as enduring the monotony, the freezing cold, and the indescribable Cariboo mud that bogged down men and machines when the weather turned mild, the men also coped with some unexpected disasters, such as the one at

Disaster hits when two bulldozers go through the ice at Anahim Lake.
(COURTESY COLIN MACDONALD)

Anahim Lake when a bulldozer went through the ice. When a second cat tried to pull out the first one, it too went through and eventually both had to be winched out.

Finally the troops reached the end of the boulder-strewn road at the top of the Precipice Trail. (Highway 20, also known as the Freedom Road, was not punched through by Bella Coola residents until 1953.)

In an interview with *Tribune* reporter Sage Birchwater a few years ago, Colin MacDonald, who was a lieutenant in charge of the Pioneer Platoon, remembered that they "just parked all the vehicles and started walking."

This was when the services of Alfred Bryant and Ulkatcho guide Thomas Squinas were called into play, he said. While Bryant guided part of the expedition down the Precipice Trail, Squinas was taking a smaller group down the Capoose Trail. "The path was pretty undistinguishable at that time of the year," recalled MacDonald.

Four miles east of Stuie, wagons and supplies were dropped from planes by parachute, and the force then proceeded to Bella Coola, 310 miles from the main base at Williams Lake.

At Bella Coola, ships of the Royal Canadian Navy were waiting to evacuate the equipment. The troops were ordered back to Prince George a week later. The men were disappointed, as they hadn't had time to really get to know the Bella Coola people, said MacDonald. "One man would even time his daughter when she went out to milk the cow," he remarked ruefully.

The final leg—plodding down the muddy hill to Bella Coola. (COURTESY COLIN MACDONALD)

The expedition proceeded back up the valley, taking a new route by way of Atnarko, Turner Trail and Slide to Anahim Lake, and eventually ending back at the base camp at Williams Lake before returning to Prince George.

But the story of the great Polar Bear Expedition doesn't end there. Ex-B.C. Policeman Bob Turnbull, who was stationed at Alexis Creek then, said that when the Bull Canyon camp was about to be closed, one of the lieutenants came and remarked, "We've dug a trench and filled it with the surplus provisions and will be burning it before we leave tomorrow."

Turnbull thought about the meaning of the message for awhile, then got busy notifying the local residents. "That trench had canned ham and butter and all kinds of rations. All night long a stream of cars went back and forth from the area. There were tons hauled out that night, and nobody ever said anything about it."

Another amusing incident involved the only two eligible girls in Anahim Lake. "Their father would hear a Jeep coming and send the girls out into the bush behind the house," Bob recalled. When the young officers would arrive, their father would regretfully announce that the girls had gone out. "If only we had a telephone, you would be able to call and make sure the girls were home," he commented slyly.

"Well, sure enough, the Army strung a phone wire for twenty miles, and it was in operation for many years," related Bob with a chuckle.

Strangely enough, although the influx of that huge contingent of men and machines must have had a tremendous impact on the economy and social life of the tiny village of Williams Lake (population around 900), I could not find a single reference to the Polar Bear scheme in back issues of the *Tribune*.

Tribune editor/publisher George Renner seems to have bent over backwards to abide by censorship regulations and didn't print a thing about the Polar Bear scheme or any other defense projects. But he wasn't too happy about it. In a 1942 editorial he complained, "What sometimes makes us hot around the collar is instruction not to mention such things as the Alaska Highway and then a week later comes radio broadcasts on the same subjects that are forbidden to us."

The Polar Bear expedition was not the only army winter training in Canada. Another, called the Eskimo Exercise, took place around the same time in northern Saskatchewan. It too was designed to test the mobility of modern formations in undeveloped country during acute cold weather.

Bare-legged women help keep army warm

Williams Lake, April 1945—Canadian Army's Polar Bear tactical exercise in rugged central British Columbia is one of the many reasons for the shortage of nylon and rayon stockings.

The six-man tents used by the soldiers have an outer layer of nylon and one lining of rayon.

—From a Vancouver daily newspaper

Only in the Cariboo

Stagecoach Memories

BX stagecoach drivers were outstanding horsemen, and Charlie Westover was one of the best—which leads me to an amusing incident that happened on one of Charlie's trips to Barkerville.

He had just started his spirited horses down a hill when they suddenly bolted. Taking his whip from its socket, he cracked the lash time and again, first near one horse, then another, racing the six horses for all that was in them, and yelling: "Run away from me, will you? Then, run! I'll show you!"

The stagecoach went swaying and careening down the long hill and out over the flats, with the passengers hanging on for dear life until at last, winded and with their sides heaving, the horses drew to a stop. Charlie then turned to a passenger beside him, saying, "Well, they won't try that again," and explaining that he had used an age-old method for breaking horses of running away.

"But," the white-faced passenger yelled in his ear, "the stagecoach was being held up."

Apparently the first warning shot from the bandit's gun as he approached from the rear had made the horses bolt. Charlie hadn't seen the bandit nor heard the gun; he thought his horses had spooked for no apparent reason. You see, he was deaf as a post.

However, the express company sent Westover a cheque for a tidy sum for preventing a holdup—even if he wasn't aware of it.

Could it have been Charlie Westover at the reins of this stagecoach on the Cariboo Road? (BCARS A-09775)

A Practical Joker

Alfred Bernard Hamilton were the names given to this man born at the 150 Mile House in 1889, but throughout the Cariboo and particularly at Lac la Hache he was known as "Buffalo"—"Buff" for short.

Buff grew to be a humped, lean, slow-of-motion man. Asthma plagued him from the cradle to the grave. There were times in his youth when his agonized gasping was thought to be his last, but the thin, wiry youngster had a way of rallying and disappointing many of his would-be-mourners. Buffalo had a facetious nature from birth.

He traced his lineage to the Orkney Islands. It was from that rugged land that his grandfather, Gavin Hamilton, had come as a youth to enlist with the Hudson's Bay Company in northern British Columbia. However, Buff wasn't greatly concerned with the importance of his forefathers. He learned to trap the coyote, mink, and muskrat. He rode and handled a horse with ease and was an expert shot until his eyesight began to fail. He was an artist with his axe, as many a log building bears witness, but he will go down in posterity mainly for his humour and the execution of practical jokes. Even his last rites lacked the usual solemnity.

Buff died in the Williams Lake hospital on December 30, 1955, and the service was set for 2:30 p.m. on Tuesday, January 3, in the Lac la Hache hall. The undertaker was scheduled to bring the coffin (and Buff) down from Williams Lake.

On Tuesday afternoon the people from the valley gathered in the hall to pay their last respects to an old friend and pioneer. It was a cold day. The wind whipped around the corners, making the zero weather feel like twenty below. The hall was cold, and the people, hoping for a short service, slipped into the icy chairs.

The organist took her place and thumbed through a book of sacred songs. The minister set up his portable pulpit. Both rubbed their numbed fingers. Everyone waited. The congregation turned hopefully each time a straggler tiptoed in. The chief mourners in the front row began to fidget.

Half an hour elapsed and the people began to mutter; some stamped around, swinging their arms briskly to get the blood circulating. By this time the little organist was swearing mad. She jumped from her icy perch and suggested that an envoy be sent to the nearest phone to check on hearse and occupants. It was plain that she had her suspicions about Buff's practical joking, dead or alive.

In twenty minutes the messenger was back with the report that the undertaker with Buff had left Williams Lake about noon. There ensued much speculation as to drifts, engine trouble, etc. The crowd was cold, anxious, and a little annoyed. It was now 3:30, and in another twenty minutes darkness would be on the land. Then just as a postponement was contemplated, in dashed the hearse at 60 miles per hour. They had been at Twilight Hotel beer parlour for more than two hours.

Of course this was not discovered until the last rites had been quickly dispensed with and Buff was tucked away under the snow. True to form, Buff had brought his facetious life to a close with this grand crescendo. Making the undertaker drunk and keeping the unhappy crowd milling about cold and impatient was a situation Buff would have split his sides over.

(Condensed from a 1956 article by the late Molly Forbes, Lac la Hache historian)

This mobile kitchen, printed with "presented by the people of Southern Cariboo to the people of Britain," helped bombed-out Britons in World War II.

The House Will Be Dry

The story of how the hard-drinking Cariboo received fame in an unusual way during World War II is one for the history books. Its residents were asked to give up liquor for Christmas!

This happened in the fall of 1940, when Williams Lake businessman Bob Beauchamp chanced to hear a radio broadcast appealing for help to provide more mobile kitchens for bombed-out Britons.

"When heating, cooking, and such facilities are destroyed," intoned the announcer, "these kitchens move right into the bombed area to provide hot meals for the homeless women and children, the air raid workers, firefighters, nurses and doctors, and all others who are suffering and working in the front line."

Beauchamp was deeply moved by the appeal, and along with concerned residents Syd Western, Harold Richardson, Bob Blair, Rod Mackenzie, and Tony Woodland quickly formed a committee to raise money for the project.

I don't know which one came up with the idea of "giving up liquor, cigars, and other indulgences" for the cause during the Christmas season, but the unique fund-raiser received nationwide recognition when it was aired over CBC Radio's *Carry on Canada* series in the fall of 1940.

Called "Christmas Box for the Bombed," the program first featured a true incident of a war-worker who risked her life to save two mobile kitchens during a raid at Southampton. Then followed a Cariboo playlet with cattlemen and miners digging down deep to buy a mobile kitchen, ending with the reading of this letter composed by the Williams Lake committee:

> We enjoy our liquor in this cattle and mining country, and especially at Christmas time when we usually celebrate in a right royal way requiring a strong stomach and a hard head. We're pledged to put into the Christmas box fund the amount of money we would otherwise spend on Christmas liquor...and expect our local vendor to have a real holiday this year to make up for the Christmases when we have so overworked him in the past. This will bring the war home to us in a very personal way, and Hitler is being damned heartily but quite cheerfully.

The letter finished off with: "So, if you stray up onto this range this Christmas, you'll be welcome as ever, but the house will be dry. Come back again when the war is won, and see what the deferred celebration will be like."

Well, that really hit home to a lot of people. Considering how few people there were in the Cariboo and Williams Lake then, the response was fantastic. Not only did they raise over $3,000 for a handsome mobile kitchen, but there was also enough left over to equip it and provide some food.

Hard-working secretary Beauchamp even expressed regret in one of his letters to Lord Woolton, Minister of Food Supply in London, that "we cannot arrange to send you some of our good beef steers."

It could only happen in the Cariboo.

A Car and a Chilcotin Tragedy

There have been many little tragedies in the history of the Cariboo-Chilcotin, and I came across this one in a most unusual way.

It concerns the sad story of Captain Jack Charters, who froze to death on a cold winter night in 1948 near Alexis Creek. I only learned of his death because he was the owner of an expensive Bentley car.

Hugh Young of Victoria, who is an historian with the Bentley Drivers Club, phoned one day to see if I had any information on Charters and his untimely death, and a search of the *Tribune* files revealed a most fascinating tale.

> With shelter almost within his grasp, Capt. Jack
> Wemyss Charters, 38-year-old British Army Reserve
> officer, died from exposure November 26 near Alexis
> Creek. His body was found not more than 300 yards
> from the old Newton ranch house by Jack Bliss.

Charters was apparently on his way to Williams Lake from his rented Chilco Lake cabin when his Willys-Jeep station wagon broke down on the lonely "bush" road. From there the captain alternately walked and ran for fourteen miles in ten below zero temperature (-24° Celsius) until he fell exhausted in the snow. Scraps of Canadian money and spent matches scattered around him were mute evidence of his futile attempts to light a fire before the freezing cold overcame him.

If there had been a light on in the Newton house, he would have been able to see it from where he fell, but Jack and June Bliss were away that evening and unaware of the tragedy taking place near their home. The next morning as Jack rode out to look for cattle, he noticed an odd bundle of clothes beside a log near his gate. Riding over to investigate he discovered Charters' body clad in a heavy sheepskin coat, half reclining against the log as though he had just stopped for a rest.

Bliss then notified B.C. Policeman Bob Turnbull at Alexis Creek who, after bringing the body into Williams Lake, contacted Daphne Charters at Vancouver and learned that her husband had driven out to their cabin to retrieve some personal effects and her unfinished paintings. Before leaving Williams Lake, he had filled his vehicle and two extra jerry cans with gas.

A recent photo of ex-B.C. Policeman Bob Turnbull.

With that little bit of information tucked away, Turnbull headed out to Chilco Lake to try and solve the mystery of Charters' fateful walk that cold winter night. On the way he stopped at Alexis Creek to pick up ex-B.C. Policeman Johnny Blatchford, who may have been the last man to see Charters alive. "He stopped and had supper with my wife and me on his way out to Chilco," Blatchford recalled, "and I cautioned him about wearing warmer clothing. But he assured us he had more in the car."

The two men followed Charters' footprints back over the snow-covered road until they found the abandoned Jeep, which had run out of gas due to a frozen air cleaner. "They were the footprints of a man in a hurry but in complete control," declares Turnbull. Then it was on to Charters' cabin. Strangely enough, they found it unlocked, the personal effects and paintings laid out to go, and a half-prepared meal on the table. In the yard were the two full jerry cans of gas.

Something clearly must have caused Charters to leave in a hurry. Did he have a dizzy spell or a warning of an impending heart attack? It remains a mystery to this day.

Described as a tall, lean, aristocratic-looking man, Charters had arrived in Canada the previous winter and worked during the summer for the International Pacific Salmon commission at Farwell Canyon in the Chilcotin. As far as was known, he was in the best of health.

Another *Tribune* report, dated January 13, 1949, and headlined "CHILCOTIN DEATH HAS STRANGE SEQUEL," tells of how on the

The mangled Bentley after the moose encounter in the Chilcotin in 1948. Owner Captain L.J. Goudy is in the car, with his daughter Elizabeth at right. (Courtesy E. Booth)

night Charters died, his dog, which was being treated for a broken leg 400 miles away in a Vancouver veterinary hospital, suddenly began howling and barking and could hardly be restrained. The next day he was completely normal and docile again.

Vintage car owners are undoubtedly wondering what happened to Charters' superb 1932 eight-litre Bentley. From items in the Bentley Car Club's quarterly *Review*, it appears Charters first registered it with the club in June 1947 at Windsor, England.

When he and his wife Daphne immigrated to Canada that winter, they drove the handsome maroon car from Halifax to the Chilcotin. It attracted admiring throngs whenever it stopped, says the *Review*, and was surely the longest "delivery flight" for any Bentley ever. It had some rough experiences in the Chilcotin from all accounts, including an "unnatural coupling with a moose" that resulted in a mangled fender.

After Charters' death, the car was purchased and restored by Captain Lawrence J. Goudy of Vancouver/Victoria, who kept it until the mid-1980s. From his daughter, Elizabeth (Goudy) Booth, comes the information that only 100 of the powerful two-ton cars were produced between 1928 and 1932, with Charters' being the 98th. "It was a huge car made of solid aluminum," says Mrs. Booth. "The moose must have lost out in the encounter."

The vintage Bentley is now owned by Reto Domeniconi of Switzerland.

Farwell Canyon

Like many others, I have often taken summer visitors out to see the stark beauty of Farwell Canyon near Riske Creek. If we're lucky, we may see yellow river-rafts full of holidayers come bouncing down the blue-green waters of the Chilcotin River, then hurtle through the narrow gorge, leaving delighted screams echoing on the afternoon breeze.

If we're lucky, we may also see native people perched precariously on the sheer rock faces dipping for salmon, a tradition that dates back to their ancestors who also fished this river. Across the bridge, evidence of their passing can be seen in a few ancient pictographs painted on a rock face up on a small plateau where we can stop to gaze with awe at the wind-eroded cliffs or "hoodoos" that surround this spectacular valley.

And we can also look down on a forlorn cluster of buildings, long abandoned, which are all that remain of the home of Gordon "Mike" Farwell for whom this canyon was named.

If you're brave enough to pick your way down the two ruts that lead to the canyon floor, you will wonder how anyone could possibly have lived there year-round. Even Farwell must have had his doubts at times.

In his memoirs he writes: "I have seen it 105° F in the shade after 6 p.m. for three nights running and it was like an oven! In the winter the sun peeped over the high bluffs for ten minutes, then disappeared." But his crops were phenomenal. "I could grow anything," he claimed.

The first settler at this small homestead, however, was Louis Vedan. Born at Empire Valley, Louis worked at ranches throughout the Cariboo-

This superb photo of the original bridge at Farwell Canyon, washed out by a slide in 1964, was taken by pioneer photographer J. Simonson in the 1920s.

Chilcotin before acquiring the land in the canyon, where the pitiless summer sun bounced off the towering cliffs, and in winter the steep treacherous road made travelling in and out almost impossible.

Dates are vague, but sometime in the early 1900s Vedan sold to Mike Farwell, a young "mudpup" who had emigrated from England in 1903. Farwell immediately dubbed his home, tucked in beside the Chilcotin River, the "Pothole Ranch," a name that has endured to this day.

Farwell noticed the great many wild horses on the range and was soon in the business of supplying horses for prospectors and buyers coming through from Alberta and Kamloops. Vedan, who was often morose and cranky, nevertheless turned out to be a "wonderful hunter and tracker," and stayed on to help Farwell for a few years.

Then in 1912 Gerald Blenkinsop, another ambitious Englishman who had come over to work at the Chilco Ranch, joined Farwell at the Pothole. It was a successful partnership that saw the two young ranchers marry and establish separate homes on the flat beside the rushing Chilcotin River—Gerald with tiny, lively "Queenie" Wheeler, and Farwell with an Irish lass by the name of Chris Riley.

Although it must have been a lonely life for the two young wives, who were seldom able to leave their isolated homes at the bottom of the precipitous canyon, there were many happy times too, in a house filled with music. Queenie was an excellent musician, and

Gerald Blenkinsop, left, and Mike Farwell share a light-hearted moment at the Cotton Ranch near Riske Creek in the early 1900s. (COURTESY CAROL HUTCHINSON)

she won over grumpy Vedan with her bright ways—so much so that he gave her a Gerhard Heintzman piano for a wedding gift, bringing it down the steep, narrow road by wagon. (In later years Queenie donated her prized piano to the Cariboo Park Home at Williams Lake, and it can still be seen there today.)

Farwell's colourful description of bringing in "the old Doc" (Wright) by sleigh and team from the Becher House at Riske Creek to attend his wife one cold moonlit night gives one some insight into the dangers of travelling the Farwell Canyon road in the early 1900s.

The good doctor, who had been celebrating his birthday not too wisely, was asleep when Farwell started his descent to the river down a hog's back with a deep gully on each side. Called "the toboggan slide," it was just wide enough for the sleigh. Farwell woke the Doc and warned him, "Hang on tight, because if you go overboard here, you'll break your neck sure."

The horses had just gone two steps when the doctor took a nose-dive over the front of the sleigh, taking Farwell with him. Fortunately the team stopped dead. In the melee, the back of the sleigh tipped up and the two men ended up under the buggy seat with an open tin of cigarettes "sprayed over us like confetti at a wedding."

"I got out of the mess almost immediately," Farwell goes on, "but the Doc was lying under the tongue between the horses, on his face and dead to the world."

The deserted Farwell home down in the canyon as it looked in 1998.

He was a big heavy man, but somehow Farwell got him out despite the black void yawning just a foot away. Dumping the Doc like a sack of potatoes in the back of the sleigh, Farwell then completed the hazardous journey to the Pothole. The next day the doctor commented, "It's a most curious thing; I've had a complete lapse of memory ever since this morning at the hotel."

Despite many similar escapades, the doctor was "one of the best," declared Farwell. "Although quite elderly, he would ride out to help anyone in the middle of winter and even sleep out in a snowbank."

In 1919 the partners sold the Pothole to the sprawling Gang Ranch, which for many years maintained it as one of their many cow camps. The two families, in the meantime, shifted to ranching in the Big Creek area, but in 1925 the Farwells decided to move to Victoria permanently. The Blenkinsops stayed and ranched in the Chilcotin until retiring to Williams Lake, where Gerald died in 1969. Bright little Queenie lived at the Cariboo Park Home until 1992, then moved to Victoria where she died four years later at 106 years of age.

Now to tell you of the more recent history of Farwell Canyon. Today, as you lean over the bridge spanning the rushing torrent, you may not realize that the cribbing fanning out at river's edge is the remains of fish ladders built between 1947 and 1949 by the International Pacific Salmon Commission.

About 25 to 30 people were employed in the joint Canada/U.S. venture. American money paid for the equipment, but the project was supervised by Canadians and well organized. The only access

Men working on the fish ladders in Farwell Canyon in the late 1940s. Remains of the ladders can still be seen today. (COURTESY EARL CAHILL)

to the site was by way of the original Farwell Canyon road, which still clung precariously to cliff edges as it jack-knifed down to a narrow, timbered bridge built in the early 1900s by the Gang Ranch.

Completed by the winter of 1949, the fishway was invaluable for many years, making it possible for salmon to navigate the narrow channel up to their spawning beds. Then suddenly on the morning of August 20, 1964, a huge chunk of hillside on the south bank thundered down, dumping five million cubic yards of earth and debris into the Chilcotin River. It was one of the biggest slides ever recorded in the province. The river rose 50 feet over its normal level, and the original bridge was swept from its moorings and wrecked. The northern approach was buried under tons of dirt. "Mud from the phenomenon was seen as far south as the mouth of the Fraser," reported the *Williams Lake Tribune.*

Many feared the salmon run would be lost, but the slide had a strange effect. After the waters subsided, it was discovered the river had been flushed out and the salmon could swim easily through the channel, so the fish ladders were no longer needed. A brand-new bridge was built a little farther upstream from the old site, accessed by a new Forestry road that dipped down to the river in long sweeping curves. Today from this vantage point you can still see the old fish ladders, a lasting bit of Chilcotin history.

And down in the Canyon is the shell of the Farwell home, a few outbuildings, and memories.

The Great Bank Robbery

Light spilled from the window of the Bank of Commerce on the corner of First and Oliver Street onto the snow-covered streets of the tiny village of Williams Lake on the night of December 15, 1952.

Inside, manager Len Hellyer was working late, unaware that he would soon be caught up in the most harrowing experience of his life, a terrifying drama that would only end twelve hours later with a shootout at the nearby Sugar Cane Reserve.

Finally putting away his papers around 11:15, Hellyer prepared to leave. Carefully locking the bank door, he got into his car parked nearby. Just as he was pulling away from the curb, a well-dressed man slipped into the passenger seat. "Going my way?" he enquired.

It was dark, and the manager could not make out the man's identity, but in a small town where violence was rare, he was unsuspecting. "It depends on where you're going," he commented as he started up Oliver Street.

"Just up the street a little way," the stranger replied.

Halfway up the first block, Hellyer felt the barrel of a gun pushed into his ribs, and his passenger growled, "This is it, fellow. This is a holdup."

The following hour was one of paralyzing fear and horror for Hellyer. The holdup man, a powerfully built six-foot chap in his late twenties, forced him to drive out towards the village dump where he outlined his plan of action. "We'll go back to the bank and you'll open the vault, then put the money in this satchel until I tell you to stop," he said, pointing to a canvas zippered bag he was carrying.

Although Hellyer tried to explain the bank safe was on a time-lock and could not be opened until morning, the would-be robber ignored his protests. When they drove back into town, a number of people were standing on the corner near the bank, and the gunman ordered Hellyer to drive on. Constantly nudging his ribs with the gun as they circled the quiet streets, the holdup man kept warning him what would happen if he didn't obey instructions.

Seeking to gain time, Hellyer falteringly remarked, "My wife will be expecting me home; she'll wonder where I am."

Bank manager Len Hellyer.
(COURTESY RUTH HELLYER)

But the robber already knew Hellyer was married and had two children and a cocker spaniel. "Do as you're told," he snapped, "and you'll be with your kids for Christmas." The man's knowledge of his family was chilling news for the manager.

The gunman then ordered him to drive out to the dump a second time, where he fired his .32 automatic into the ground, warning Hellyer, "Now you see I mean business—and you wouldn't be the first one." It sounded ominous to Hellyer, but it wasn't until much later that he learned this was no small-time thief, but a man already wanted for murder.

Relieving the manager of his wallet, the gunman then ordered him to return to the bank once more. Throughout the nightmarish ride, Hellyer desperately tried to devise some means of attracting attention, but his only hope was that Doug Adair, the young teller who lived above the bank, might hear them when they returned.

This time the street was deserted, and with the gunman still threatening him with the gun, Hellyer unlocked the bank's outside door with shaking fingers, leaving it slightly ajar as instructed. As they moved past the teller's cages in the dimly lit bank, Hellyer again protested that the inner safe could not be opened until morning, but the robber merely snarled, "Hurry it up."

The Bank of Commerce, right, on the corner of Oliver Street and First Avenue as it looked in the 1950s. The RCMP offices and jail were in the courthouse, left. (COURTESY MARY O'DONOVAN)

Nervously Hellyer spun the tumblers and slowly pulled open the heavy vault door, all the time praying for a miracle. Suddenly there came a rattling sound at the front door, and the gunman spun around to see two men entering.

Bank accountant Don Mars and local businessman Tony Kallaur had stopped for a late coffee at the nearby Famous Cafe following a Legion meeting, and they were on their way home when they noticed the bank door ajar. Although they didn't suspect anything was seriously wrong, they decided to investigate. Even when a voice from the shadows barked, "This is a holdup! Put up your hands," they thought at first it was some kind of practical joke.

The gunman next manoeuvred himself between the men and the door, then ordered Hellyer to move up too. As the manager neared the counter, the gunman opened fire without a moment's warning. The bullet entered Hellyer's abdomen two inches below his navel, going right through and exiting just half an inch from his spine.

As the manager sagged to the floor, the robber bolted out the door and disappeared into the darkness. Despite his wound, Hellyer managed to press the Alert button for the police across the street.

In her home a few blocks away, Ruth Hellyer was becoming increasingly concerned about her husband's lateness. Phoning the bank, she asked Adair if Len was still working. "No," came the shocking reply, "he's been shot. He's in hospital." Although he was

Marius Mortenson tracked the gunman for the RCMP, who then cornered and captured him.
(COURTESY *WILLIAMS LAKE TRIBUNE*)

just upstairs, the young teller had not heard a thing until the shot rang out.

The gunman by this time was frantically trying to escape his pursuers as he zig-zagged through the countryside, doubling back and forth through gullies, creek beds, and logging roads, and even walking along barbed wire fences and climbing trees in his efforts to shake off the Mounties' search parties headed by Sergeant Joe Howe.

It was the biggest manhunt Williams Lake has ever seen—either before or since that time. Police poured in from Kamloops, 100 Mile, Alexis Creek, and Quesnel to take up the chase, with veteran predator animal hunter Marius Mortenson finally being brought in at 4 a.m. His trained eyes proved invaluable for following the trail, which often petered out on bare frozen ground.

It wasn't until 10:30 in the morning, after eight hours of cold, slow, tedious tracking, that the desperado was cornered in a clump of willows in a creek bottom just past the Sugar Cane Reserve south of Williams Lake by three RCMP headed by Constable William G. Pooler of Quesnel.

When their quarry suddenly loomed up with his automatic pointed at Pooler's stomach, the men flung themselves down—and a short but deadly battle was on. It ended when the bandit collapsed with a gunshot wound in the chest.

News of the spectacular hunt and capture at Williams Lake was plastered on the front pages of newspapers throughout the country, but there was more to come. Six days later police were stunned to receive word from RCMP headquarters that their prisoner had been identified as Henry Seguin, wanted for the murder of taxi-driver Leonard Hurd of Maxville, Ontario, just four months earlier. "EXERCISE EXTREME CAUTION AS SEGUIN VERY DANGEROUS," read the telegram.

Seguin had started his life of crime at the tender age of ten, and his convictions included everything from break-ins to robbery with violence. He had just been released from Kingston Penitentiary in

February. Pleading guilty to all charges at Williams Lake, he was sentenced to three 15- to 20-year sentences to run concurrently.

Then the Ontario Police stepped into the picture with a warrant for his return to Kingston to stand trial for Hurd's murder. On October 29 he was found guilty and sentenced to hang on January 19, 1954. But this time Seguin foiled his hunters. About an hour before he was scheduled to walk the thirteen steps to the scaffold, he committed suicide by swallowing potassium cyanide. How he obtained the vial of poison was never known.

The story doesn't end there. In September 1955 a three-year-old mystery was solved when the bones of Frederick and Jeanne Labrie were found at the bottom of a ravine on a farm near Kamloops. There was a bullet hole in one skull. The couple was believed to have been murdered by Henry Seguin, who had lived with the Labries before moving to Williams Lake. Investigators discovered Seguin had sold about $1,000 worth of their furniture and sold or traded their truck.

And so the notorious Seguin case finally wound to a close.

But it didn't end for Len Hellyer, who never fully recovered from his nightmarish experience. "It definitely shortened his life," said his wife, Ruth. "He was never the same." After an extended leave, the manager worked in Vancouver branches of the bank until 1958, when he retired because of health problems. He died in 1970; his widow in 1999.

Birth of a Hospital

Raising money to build a hospital in the new village of Williams Lake could be a wild-and-woolly affair, according to a letter Bank of Commerce manager Louis Dallaire sent to his head office in February 1920.

Describing a weekend dance held in the nearly completed Fraser and Mackenzie store, Dallaire writes: "About 150 people made merry Friday night, but Saturday was the big day for gamblers. Some were very weird characters playing anything, anywhere; on tables or on the floor, trading away horses, saddles, accoutrements, fur coats etc.

Dancing started at ten o'clock but the big show began at midnight when a train came in bringing a number of outsiders and a generous supply of liquor. It was not long before everybody was pretty well under. One man had to be ejected and when the crowd followed him out, the doors were locked and they were left to fight it out among themselves. Nobody was killed.

"Everybody had a 'pleasant' time," he finishes, "and we think this will be a good advertisement for Williams Lake. We cleared about $275 for the hospital fund."

It would take several years of fund-raising before Williams Lake got its first real hospital in 1925. In the meantime, Nora Weetman, RN, operated a small two-bed nursing home cum emergency hospital near the foot of Oliver Street.

When the time came in 1924 to pick the site for a hospital, several businessmen took PGE agent Bob Wark up Oliver Street and pointed to a big cottonwood that topped a hill south of town. "Bob, we want you to give us those five acres for the hospital."

The War Memorial Hospital in the 1930s after a seventeen-bed wing had been added on, right.

Bob demurred at first, saying there was no way the railway would "give" them the land, but a deal was finally struck. The selling price was one dollar.

That first little cottage hospital perched on the hill "way out of town" (now the site of city hall) was built for $11,050. There was one private room and two small wards downstairs, two wards upstairs, and a large verandah. Called the War Memorial Hospital, the name was chosen because of Soda Creek's contribution. Prior to Williams Lake's "birth" in 1919, Soda Creek was still a bustling road and sternwheeler terminus, and its residents had been raising money to build a cenotaph to honour their World War I dead. But when the PGE's ribbon of steel reached Williams Lake and it became the "Hub of the Cariboo," the fund was turned over to help build a more fitting memorial—a hospital in the new village.

First resident doctor at Williams Lake was Irish-born Dr. Francis Vere Agnew, who after immigrating to Canada became company doctor in 1914 for the PGE Railway during its original construction period. Dr. Agnew stuck with the railroad until it reached the Williams Lake area, then established his own practice.

A tall cheerful young man, just in his 30s, with a rich speaking voice, he must have had some incredible experiences during his eight years in the Cariboo. At one particularly riotous Stampede he remarked, "I tend the sick, but I think the good Lord tends the cowboys," after watching the plunging front hooves of a bucking bronc narrowly miss a fallen cowboy's head.

Dr. Agnew left Williams Lake in 1928 and two years later settled at Smithers, where he practised until his death at 52 years. His first wife, Maida, died at Williams Lake in 1921 and is buried at St. Joseph's Mission cemetery.

Government help for hospitals was minimal in those days. In Williams Lake whist drives, dances, and plays were constantly being staged to raise money. The hospital produced hundreds of pounds of vegetables every year in its own garden, and the Hospital Auxiliary women would buy up bolts of material and, using treadle machines and sad irons heated on wood stoves, make it up into sheets, pillowcases, gowns, and layettes. The annual Pound Day also brought in lots of donations.

Pound Day? I can almost hear my readers asking, "What on earth was Pound Day?" I'm not sure when it originated, but on National Hospital Day residents brought in everything from

Dr. Hugh Atwood, in the 1950s, with his trademark cigarette in one hand, stethescope in the other.
(COURTESY HUGH ATWOOD)

foodstuffs and garden produce to linens and money to help keep the hospital running. The custom petered out in the late 1950s, about the time government started funding hospital services.

The war years brought many problems to the little hospital, which by now had expanded with a seventeen-bed wing and babies' ward. In September 1942 it had to close when the only doctor left town. Staff shortages were also a continuing headache, and even board members pitched in from time to time to keep the hospital open. On one occasion Florie Woodland took over the kitchen, did all the cooking, and enlisted her husband, Tony, and two sons, Roy and Ralph, to help as orderlies and to bring in wood for the big kitchen stove, furnace, and laundry.

Many dedicated doctors have ministered to the ills of Williams Lake and the Cariboo-Chilcotin over the years, and their experiences would fill a book. You just have to listen to the tales spun by retired physician Hugh Atwood, who at 84 is Williams Lake's

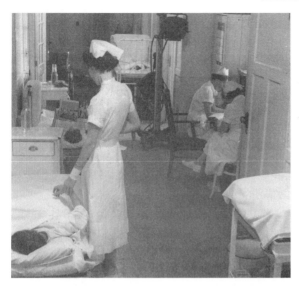

Corridor of the overcrowded War Memorial Hospital in 1959. (COURTESY *WILLIAMS LAKE TRIBUNE*)

oldest resident doctor—in both years and service—to get some conception of their tremendous workload and the difficulties of coping with inadequate facilities.

When he arrived in Williams Lake in 1952, Dr. Atwood anticipated a more leisurely career in the little village (population 1,000) than he had known in big city hospitals. But his dream was short-lived. The only other doctor, Larry Avery, who had served the community for eight years, left for a new career in the U.S., and the new physician was suddenly faced with an exploding practice fuelled by the booming lumber industry.

In some desperation he contacted a wartime friend, a surgeon he had worked with in an overseas hospital, and persuaded him to leave Edmonton for the wilds of the Cariboo. His name was Barney Ringwood, and the next ten years would see the partners grapple with a 28-bed facility that was woefully inadequate for the demands.

"We were running at 140 percent capacity at one time and had the highest birth rate in Canada. I delivered five babies one day, four another, and had lots of threes and twos," recalled Dr. Atwood. Some of the babies were placed in orange boxes, others in dresser drawers brought down from Matron Eva Lockwood's room upstairs.

There was no maternity ward, and the operating room was used for everything from emergencies and major surgery to deliveries and examinations. A trip to the one bathroom for patients sometimes entailed winding your way through eight people lying on stretchers and mattresses in the hallway. "We even had two on a mattress one time," Dr. Atwood recalled. "A chap came in from Horsefly with a minor injury. There were no beds and we figured he would have to go home. But he knew one of the men lying in the hallway, and they agreed to bunk together."

With the addition of a 10-bed maternity ward in 1955, the hospital expanded to 40 beds, but it was still very overcrowded. That wasn't the only problem. There was no ambulance service by road or air, so seriously ill or injured patients had to be transported to Vancouver riding on a mattress in the back of someone's station wagon, a trip that could take twelve hours—even more when the roads were clogged by blizzards. Usually one of the doctors went along. And of course they thought nothing of making house calls into the country; it was part of the job. "I worked until seven or eight o'clock at night, then did ten or twelve house calls; sometimes I didn't get to sleep at all," Dr. Atwood related.

Dr. Atwood had high praise for the nursing staff in those "primitive" years. "They were wonderful; there was a sense of community and they would often stay on after their regular shift if necessary," he contended. "Of course the paper work was non-existent then; today it is tremendous—just pages and pages about nothing."

On August 24, 1962, Williams Lake's best-loved and highly respected physician cut the ribbon at the official opening of the new Cariboo Memorial Hospital. With his usual easy humour, he likened it to the birth of a baby. "When this beautiful new offspring was born, the mother and all the assembled people looked at this thing they had brought forth, and as so often is the case, they said, 'Well, the heartburn, the backaches, and even the haemorrhoids were worth it.'"

Today Dr. Atwood, who has stayed to see many of his "babies" grow up to adulthood and have children and grandchildren, still looks back with fondness on his early days in Williams Lake. "I loved the old hospital," he says with great nostalgia. " It was like an old house that went on and on. Those were the good days; I wouldn't have missed them for the world."

Mountain Race

The famous Mountain Race, a frightening breakneck dash down Fox Mountain, high above the present Overlander Hotel, to the Stampede grounds, was the exciting climax of every Stampede, starting in 1922 until the last race was run in 1953.

This story is about Pierro Squinahan, the man who won the Mountain Race more times than any other rider, and his mysterious disappearance many years later.

Pierro was born around October 15, 1899, at Alkali Lake and later worked at Springhouse, Dog Creek, and the Alkali Lake Ranch as a cowboy and ranch-hand.

A small, slim man, he learned to ride extremely well, so it was inevitable he should compete in the Williams Lake Stampede as well as other rodeos around the Cariboo. "We used to travel in by wagon with a team of horses," said his widow, Lilly, whom I talked to in her neat little house on the Alkali Lake Reserve some years ago. "We would camp out—anywhere there was a rodeo."

She particularly remembered the tents ringing the amphitheatre at Williams Lake, cooking on the open fires, and getting water from the creek. "We really enjoyed it. It was all local cowboys then, and people sat on the hillside to watch. People were free to do what they wanted. There are too many rules today. You can't make fires, and there's no room left."

"Many white people used to come down and sit around the campfires with us," she recalled, "and talk and talk and talk." Many played lahal, an Indian gambling game in which bones are hit on

Pierro Squinahan in his "colours," coming in first in the Mountain Race sometime in the late 1930s or 1940s. (COURTESY LILLY SQUINAHAN)

sticks. "Twelve or more would be on a side and the money would pile up in the middle."

Lilly was born at Alkali Lake too, and went to school at the Cariboo Indian Residential School at St. Joseph's Mission for nine years, only going home for the month of August. "Some call the school down," she said, "but I was happy there. I learned to cook and sew—lots of things—and I was treated well."

The Indian children were not allowed to use their native language, but she says simply, "We learned English faster that way." Lilly and Pierro were married at St. Joseph's Mission in 1934 and continued to live at Alkali Lake, bringing up their three children.

Looking back, it was the rodeo events in which Pierro competed that stood out in her memory, particularly the 1926 Mountain Race when the riders bunched up on the ridge. The first horse fell, and the rest stumbled over it, piling up on the trail. In the melee, several horses and riders were injured, including Pierro. "He had the scars on his face for the rest of his life," said Lilly.

Pierro won the Mountain Race eight times, usually mounted on Morning Plume, the magnificent three-quarter thoroughbred that he and Joe Dick and Matthew Dick owned between them, wearing his own "racing colours" or jockey outfit. He also competed in flat races and the Roman Race (standing on two horses) and sometimes beat the legendary Bill Twan, who was famed for his prowess in that event.

The Mountain Race was phased out in 1954 when the Cariboo Highway was paved and it became too dangerous for horse and rider to cross the blacktop. At that time Pierro was presented with the handsome Mountain Race trophy in recognition of the many times he had won the famed race over the years. The family later donated it to the Museum of the Cariboo-Chilcotin.

The sad ending to my story came many years later. On October 31, 1972, the Squinahans were in Williams Lake on their way to a funeral at Canim Lake. Pierro went off with some friends and Lilly never saw him again.

Pierro Squinahan of Alkali Lake, who won the gruelling Mountain Race eight times.
(COURTESY LILLY SQUINAHAN)

"We looked and looked. We walked the road from Alkali to Williams Lake, along the river to Lillooet, up to Soda Creek, and circled Williams Lake..."

He was never found.

Note: The Mountain Race was revived in 1992, but with a difference. In today's scaled-down version, the riders race down a zig-zag trail on a hillside inside the Stampede grounds, again providing an exciting finish to the day's events as it did over 70 years ago.

Names—Names—Still More Place Names

Anderson and Seton Lakes
Named for Alexander Caulfield Anderson, the explorer who was commissioned by Governor James Douglas in 1858 to open a route via Harrison Lake and Lillooet to the interior. Seton Lake, on the same route, honours his old friend and "near-relative" Colonel Alexander Seton.

Duffey Lake
This lake, and the road, is named for Sapper James Duffey, who was one of the Royal Engineers exploring a route between Lillooet and Pemberton in 1861.

One-Eye Lake
This Chilcotin lake near Kleena Kleene is named for old Chief One-Eye, who was buried on the north side of the lake in 1911.

Bull Canyon
In early days, ranchers in the Alexis Creek area used to put a drift fence at each end of the narrow canyon to pen in their bulls, making it a natural pasture.

Guy's Mountain
Named for early settler Francois "Frank" Guy, a French-Canadian packer who operated the Beaver Lake House and ranch in partnership with Ah Tom from 1870 to 1898.

Potato Mountain
This mountain near Tatlayoko Lake is now called T'Slos Nuit for the Indian chief and his wife who, according to legend, left Lillooet many moons before the white man came, and trekked north carrying wild potatoes for their long journey, planting the tiny tubers wherever they camped.

An Historic Subdivision

When Williams Lake lawyer Mike D'Arcy and his partner Dr. Peter Culbert developed a new subdivision on the Dog Creek Road near Williams Lake back in the 1970s, they decided to name the streets after historical B.C. figures.

Gun-An-Noot Trail

Simon Peter Gun-an-noot was born at Kispiox, B.C., and grew up to be an excellent hunter and trapper. Accused of the murder of two men at a small tavern near Hazelton, he took to the wilds where for thirteen long years he lived in canyons and caverns—the object of the most famous manhunt in B.C. history. He finally gave himself up, stood trial, and was acquitted. He died in 1933.

Cataline Drive

Jean Caux came from the Spanish province of Catalonia (hence his nickname) to the Cariboo in the 1860s and performed many prodigious feats of pack-train transportation, making his last trip in 1913. A colourful and rugged individual, Cataline made his winter headquarters at Dog Creek and was often observed taking an early morning bath in the snow. A school in Williams Lake is named for this early packer.

Willoughby Place

Richard Willoughby was one of those intrepid miners who found his way to the Barkerville gold fields in the 1860s. He made a sensational strike on Lowhee Creek, taking out $10,000 to $12,000 in gold the first year. He sold two years later, but mining continued at the Lowhee for over 100 years, yielding well over $2.5 million.

Waddington Trail

In 1862 a remarkable Victoria engineer by the name of Alfred Waddington felt that an inexpensive route could be constructed from Bute Inlet through the Chilcotin to the Cariboo gold fields. In the spring of 1864, Chilcotin Indians murdered most of his crew at Tragedy Canyon, and that, coupled with the incredibly awful terrain, spelled an end to the undertaking. Waddington Mountain and Canyon are also named for this early entrepreneur.

Begbie Crescent

Matthew Baillie Begbie is, of course, the famous "hanging judge," who with firmness, impartiality, and sheer force of personality maintained law and order in mining camps during the great Cariboo gold rush. He went on to become chief justice of B.C. and was eventually knighted for his work in the courts.

A Remnant of Chinook

Some of our Cariboo-Chilcotin place names, and indeed many words used regularly in conversation, reflect the Chinook language, which had its beginnings with the Tschinuks (Chinook) tribe in what is now known as Oregon. In the early 1800s there were probably 35 to 40 different native dialects in the Pacific Northwest, so communication was difficult. This set the stage for the development of a trading language, a mixture of English, French, and aboriginal languages called "Chinook." There was nothing like it anywhere else in North America, and for Hudson's Bay Company fur traders it was a tremendous help in dealing with the many tribes that peopled British Columbia. Until its demise after World War I, it is estimated that 250,000 people spoke the jargon.

Some local Chinook names include **Tyee Lake**—tyee means "chief"; **Canim Lake**—canim means "canoe"; **Nesika School** in Williams Lake—nesika means "we, us, our" interchangeably.

In other parts of B.C. we have **Cultus Lake**—cultus originally meant "idle, foolish," but now it is construed as "bad"; **Boston Bar**—the word "Boston" referred generally to Americans; **Snass Creek**—snass means "rain"; and **Skookumchuck**, meaning "turbulent water." We are speaking Chinook when we use such terms as "a skookum fellow" and "the salt chuck," and of course "tillicum," which means "friend" or "people."

The Little Train That Could

There are many humorous stories told about the old Pacific Great Eastern Railway, or BC Rail as we know it today, and one of my favourites concerns Chilcotin pioneer Agnes "Gan-Gan" Lee, who boarded the train at Squamish one day in 1919.

The railway was still under construction, so travel was slow. As the train clacked along the rough roadbed and trembled over creaking wooden trestles, Gan-Gan began knitting a pair of socks. Six times during the night the train went off the tracks, and each time the crew members staged a small celebration when they got it back on the rails again. So it was not surprising that Gan-Gan was able to hand the finished socks to the conductor as a gift when she finally reached the end of the line at Williams Lake the next day.

It was not surprising either that for many years the railway was the brunt of countless jokes and was often referred to as the Please Go Easy, Past God's Endurance, and Prince George Eventually.

But it was a unique and friendly railroad where everyone knew one another, where the engineer would stop most anywhere for passengers, to drop off a store order at an isolated homestead, or to pick up a fresh pie or cake for the crew from a grateful resident. One engineer who was also a trapper used to stop now and again along the way to see if he had caught anything.

Despite the facetious and sometimes derogatory remarks, however, there is no doubt the railway opened up the country and was the economic lifeline that brought industry, people, and jobs to the Cariboo and eventually to northern B.C. In fact, without the PGE Railway there would be no Williams Lake as we know it today.

Using massive equipment, Northern Construction workers lay the roadbed for the new Pacific Great Eastern Railway near Alexandria in 1920. (BCARS D-02964)

So how did this fledgling railway, travelling one of the world's most scenic routes, get the prestigious name "Pacific Great Eastern Railway"? It certainly wasn't great, nor eastern.

The PGE line was originally planned in 1912 to run from North Vancouver to Prince George, there to link up with the Grand Trunk Pacific. Financial backing was arranged in England with Great Eastern Railway interests—thus the name.

Soon after construction got underway, it became evident the rugged terrain along Howe Sound would present tremendous difficulties, so the main thrust was started at Squamish, then known as Newport. By 1915 the line reached Lillooet, and by the following year, Clinton. Unfortunately the contractors ran out of money, and that plus the outbreak of World War I brought construction to a halt.

In 1918 the provincial government took over and hired the Northern Construction Company to complete the line. By the summer of 1919, Premier John Oliver and his surveyors had laid out the streets for the new village of Williams Lake in the bare stubble that had once been pioneer William Pinchbeck's rich wheat fields, and in September the first PGE work train arrived.

Ethel Slater, whose husband Walter was the government-appointed caretaker for the proposed townsite, described the scene: "Then came the thrill and excitement of a lifetime, the first whistle and bell of the PGE engine as it rounded the bend from the Onward Ranch a few miles along the lake. Every man and his dog in the Cariboo seemed to have congregated for the great event—coming from Chilcotin, Soda Creek, Quesnel, and ranches near and far."

Native people were doubly excited; many had never seen a train before and followed along as the rails were laid to the foot of the lake, where the stockyards would soon be located.

The railroad eliminated the need for long, gruelling trail drives to Ashcroft, and the cattle industry became the backbone of the town's economy for the next 40-odd years, earning Williams Lake the title "Cattle Capital of B.C.," or as some were wont to say, "Biggest Bull-Shippers in the Province."

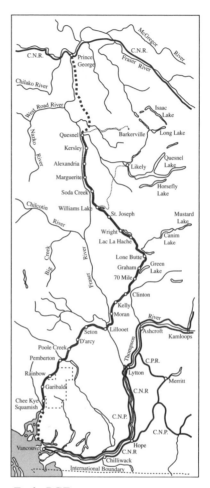

Early PGE route map. (Created from timetable supplied by John Roberts)

The next tremendous obstacle was spanning Deep Creek with huge trestles, which at 312 feet made it one of the highest railway bridges in Canada. The PGE finally reached Quesnel in 1921, and there the little railway foundered again from lack of money and interest.

For the next 30 years the PGE, which started at Squamish and ended at Quesnel, became known as "the railway that started nowhere and went nowhere," and the stories of its easy-going schedule, its antiquated rolling stock, and its many mishaps grew

*The busy PGE railroad yards and little village of Williams Lake in the
1920s. Notice the man and little girl walking the tracks.* (BCARS D-00078)

with the years. No wonder it prompted one new manager to
comment, "You stand a chance to rebuild a business that is looked
on as a tragedy, but you can't do much with a comedy."

The pioneer railway endured many hardships and tragedies in
a time when rockslides were a way of life. A summer storm one day
in August 1944 brought rocks tumbling onto the tracks south of
Lillooet, and although engineer Mike Powell tried to stop, the
locomotive hit the slide and plunged into Anderson Lake. Powell
and fireman Mulhern drowned.

Then on January 23, 1950, during one of the worst winters on
record, a small slide covered the rails south of Craig's Lodge on Seton
Lake. Coming up on it suddenly, engineer Alex Munro applied the
emergency brake, but he too was unable to stop the train's momentum.
It struck the slide, rode up on it, and slid sideways into the icy waters,
taking Munro and fireman Harry Seymour to their deaths.

When I boarded the train at Squamish in mid-February 1950 for
my first trip on the PGE, I knew nothing about the little railroad or
the recent terrible accident, so it didn't occur to me to be worried or
nervous. I slept blissfully in my berth, unaware we were held up several
times during the night for slides and were running five hours late.

The next morning passengers huddled together discussing the
previous night's events. "I was so scared," said one woman, "I almost
got out and walked."

I love the stories told by *Vancouver Herald* writer Roland Wild, who
rode with veteran engineer Charlie Midnight of Williams Lake in the
early 1950s when the PGE's slogan was "The railroad with a personality."

Veteran PGE engineer Charlie Midnight in the cab of his engine(left); and, below, his last run in 1970 into Williams Lake with a Budd Car after 50 years with the railroad (COURTESY CHERYL PROCTER)

Wild writes: "The train pulls out three times weekly from Squamish at some time agreeable to the engineer, the station-master and passengers, but usually the hour advertised in the folders of the PGE Railway Co., the loneliest and most-loved railroad in North America."

Lost in the wilderness of the Cariboo, the train chuffs along over a track suspended over chasms, then ambles gently through ranch country. But what it lacks in speed it makes up in service. Charlie will stop at the drop of a Stetson, and if he spots a moose near the track, everything comes to a halt so everyone can get a good look. Occasionally the passengers step off and play makeshift baseball just to rib the engineer over his two-mile-an-hour progress.

There are other handicaps. The route from the dining car to the front sleeping coaches leads right through the centre of the men's washroom. And to take advantage of the magnificent scenery, the top was lopped off a day coach to make an observation car— no domes of glass and such folderols for this railroad.

With men like Charlie Midnight in control, there will always be color. When spring comes, Charlie comes bustling down the line with his engine blooming with lilacs, his cab a bower of perfume.

It wasn't until 1949 that work began again to extend the PGE north from Quesnel. Finally on November 1, 1952, a jubilant Premier W.A.C. Bennett rode the first official train into Prince George, 40 years behind schedule. As Railways Minister Ralph Chetwynd stepped off the train, he intoned: "Prince George, Egad!" It was probably the last of the many humorous terms composed from the railway's initials.

Another long-awaited "missing link" was the opening of the southern extension from North Vancouver to Squamish in 1956, thus eliminating the boat ride by Union Steamships from Vancouver to Squamish.

After that it was full steam ahead for the little railroad as it launched into one of the most aggressive railway expansions of the twentieth century, extending into the Peace River country to Mackenzie, Fort St. James, and to Fort St. John by 1971.

On April 1, 1972, just a few months before his retirement, Premier W.A.C. Bennett renamed the railroad the British Columbia Railway Company; in 1984 it became simply BC Rail Ltd., and the old Please Go Easy stigma was gone for good. Gone too were the steam engines, replaced by diesels pulling modern, comfortable Budd cars. The only relic of the past is CPR's magnificent Royal Hudson steam locomotive, which puffs its way every summer from North Vancouver to Squamish and back, carrying over 100,000 awe-struck tourists from all over the world.

Today BC Rail is the interior's number one carrier and will continue to be the dominant form of transportation for its major industries for many decades to come.

The PGE
Station House

Only two of the original PGE station houses built in the province during the construction of the railway survive today. The oldest and best preserved is the one at Williams Lake, which is also the oldest "heritage" building in the city. The other is at Quesnel.

After the arrival of the PGE's first work train at Williams Lake in September 1919, the crews were immediately put to work building a bridge over Williams Lake Creek, followed by the depot at the foot of Oliver Street. On a bitterly cold day in January 1920, the first train pulled into the new station. There was no fanfare; just a few villagers and Fred Hutchinson, the first station agent and only staff member, were there to greet it.

Fred, like many of the station agents who followed, lived in the apartment above the station, which baked in summer and was difficult to heat in severe winters. When the big steam engines went through, the whole building would shake, and dishes rattled in cupboards. The bathroom for both men and women was an outside privy beside the tracks, designed to serve the travelling public and the station agent and his family.

But that wasn't good enough for one woman. When Ted Howard-Gibbons was appointed station agent in 1928, his wife Elizabeth vowed she wouldn't move to her new home unless better facilities were provided. So washrooms were installed on the east side of the station house—one downstairs for passengers and the other upstairs for the agent's family.

"We had the second bathtub in town," says daughter Libby Abbott, who recalled with great nostalgia the sixteen years her family lived in sight and sound of the busy PGE yards.

The PGE depot at Williams Lake in the early 1920s, with the controversial outside privy at left. (BCARS E-09986)

The depot, with its surrounding freight sheds, roundhouse, and water tower, was the heart of the village. The PGE supplied water for the town, school-board meetings were held in the depot, and children regularly played on and under the big platform.

Austin Howard-Gibbons remembered how his father worked from eight to five, six days a week, but still was expected to give service in off hours if someone came knocking at the door. "During the Stampede, they [PGE] used to bring up old sleeping cars and rent berths to visitors as there wasn't enough hotel accommodation."

The arrival of the weekly train was a big event, and the entire population would rush down to see who was arriving or leaving. This led to a disastrous fire in 1921, when a young woman left an iron on in her haste. The blaze wiped out half the business district and claimed the lives of two young men (see *Looking Back at the Cariboo-Chilcotin*).

Claude Pigeon, who built one of the first houses in the tiny village, got the first mail contract, but sometimes there was so little mail that he used a wheelbarrow, rather than his horse-drawn wagon, to trundle it from the PGE station over to the post office in Mackenzie's store.

The depot remained the focus for much of the town's activity until the 1960s, when the administration, freight, and daily operation offices were moved to a new complex on Bagshaw Road, leaving just the passenger waiting room in the old station. The depot by this time was in a deplorable state, with several little lean-to additions, and was termed "a blot on the landscape."

In 1981 concerned citizens applied to BC Rail for a lease on the historic building to develop it as a home for the arts in Williams Lake. Since then the Station House Studio and Gallery Society has renovated and transformed the depot until it is now one of the top tourist attractions in the city, housing the only public art gallery as well as a gift shop featuring local arts and crafts.

Note: The oldest structure still in existence from early PGE construction is the water tower built in 1916 at Lone Butte.

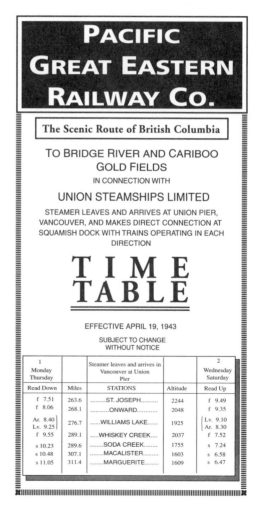

PACIFIC GREAT EASTERN RAILWAY CO.

The Scenic Route of British Columbia

TO BRIDGE RIVER AND CARIBOO GOLD FIELDS

IN CONNECTION WITH

UNION STEAMSHIPS LIMITED

STEAMER LEAVES AND ARRIVES AT UNION PIER, VANCOUVER, AND MAKES DIRECT CONNECTION AT SQUAMISH DOCK WITH TRAINS OPERATING IN EACH DIRECTION

TIME TABLE

EFFECTIVE APRIL 19, 1943

SUBJECT TO CHANGE
WITHOUT NOTICE

1 Monday Thursday		Steamer leaves and arrives in Vancouver at Union Pier		2 Wednesday Saturday
Read Down	Miles	STATIONS	Altitude	Read Up
f 7.51	263.6	.........ST. JOSEPH..........	2244	f 9.49
f 8.06	268.1	...........ONWARD...........	2048	f 9.35
Ar. 8.40 Lv. 9.25	276.7	......WILLIAMS LAKE......	1925	Lv. 9.10 Ar. 8.30
f 9.55	289.1	....WHISKEY CREEK....	2037	f 7.52
s 10.23	289.6	........SODA CREEK........	1755	s 7.24
s 10.48	307.1	........MACALISTER........	1603	s 6.58
s 11.05	311.4	........MARGUERITE........	1609	s 6.47

1943 PGE timetable.
(BASED ON PGE
TIMETABLE SUPPLIED BY
JOHN ROBERTS)

The Day We Hanged
W.A.C. Bennett

In a preceding chapter I mentioned the historic day in September 1919 when the first PGE train arrived at Williams Lake, but now I'm going to tell you about another time and another PGE train, one that involved holdups, hangings, and dance-hall girls.

In August 1956, when the link between North Vancouver and Squamish was finally completed, a special train loaded with dignitaries travelled from the coast to Prince George to celebrate the great occasion.

The train was scheduled to stop at Williams Lake for only two hours, but it was a two-hour stop that Premier W.A.C. Bennett, railways minister Ralph Chetwynd, and PGE manager Einar Gunderson would never forget.

The shenanigans started at the public beach on South Lakeside. Seven holdup men touched off 24 railroad torpedoes, and the special train ground to a halt. Three of the masked desperadoes (Tom Madison, Bert Roberts, and Bill Sharpe) jumped aboard, brandished their revolvers, and apprehended the three VIPs, who were then hustled into a BX stagecoach. With Claude Huston at the reins, they endured a bone-rattling three-mile ride in to the depot.

There the accused were marched up to a makeshift gallows, outsize nooses affixed around their necks, and the charges read by Sheriff Frank "Woody" Woodward. "I charge you PGE riding varmints with disturbing the peace in our once quiet town, cluttering up our railway track with trains and engines, also making it unsafe for cows or cowboys to sleep on the right-of-way."

PGE manager Einar Gunderson, left, Premier W.A.C. Bennett, centre, and railways minister Ralph Chetwynd guarded by deputies Tom Madison, Bill Sharpe, and Bert Roberts hear charges read by Sheriff Frank Woodward. (COURTESY WILLIAMS LAKE TRIBUNE)

They were found guilty, naturally, but Cariboo folk are basically a kindly lot and they decided to let the condemned men rest their feet awhile in the Rat Trap Saloon before they were hanged.

The nearby Central Service Garage had been transformed into an old-time barroom, complete with sawdust floor. The big hit of the day was the dancing girls, headed by queen of the dive Edie Baker as the "Lady known as Lou." Without doubt they were the most photographed women in North America that day as dozens of news cameras, reporters, and visitors flocked into the saloon.

Bartender Tom Hawker was all togged out in striped shirt and handlebar moustache, and the bill-of-fare listed such drinks as the "PGE Slowball" and "Cariboo Calamity." Big WANTED posters covered the walls. Under Bennett's picture it read: "Wanted—Whispering Ac(e) Bennett, half alive or half dead. Reward for either half 5,000,000 Socred dollars (17-1/2 cents Canadian)."

Chetwynd's poster took several jibes at his balding pate. Listed as "Curley 'Please Go Easy' Chetwynd," he was charged with breach of the easy way of Cariboo life by bringing in a railway, and of rustling Socred cows. Reward—two passes to the 1928 Stampede.

"Run Again" Gunderson was also charged with conduct contrary to the Cariboo way: "In making a business pay, not equipping trains

The gals from the Rat Trap Saloon entertained the condemned men: from left to right, Barb Poirier, Ralph Chetwynd, "Willie" Blair, Einar Gunderson, Marj Margetts, Edie Baker (the Lady known as Lou), W.A.C. Bennett, and Thelma Rife. (COURTESY WILLIAMS LAKE TRIBUNE)

with bar-rooms." The reward for him was one mounted head of rare Sacred Cow.

Everybody had a wonderful time; in fact the visitors were so taken with the entertainment that the Rat Trap Saloon almost lost Lou and bartender Hawker. When everybody flocked back to the train at departure time, the two were hustled on board and only managed to escape near the cemetery by pulling the emergency cord. They walked back to town.

And this all happened at eight o'clock in the morning! The train was scheduled to stop at Williams Lake the previous afternoon, but a rockslide north of Horseshoe Bay held it up for 22 hours. This didn't surprise the local enthusiasts, who were used to the vagaries of the PGE, and the show organized by the local Board of Trade went on as scheduled.

No wonder Williams Lake had a reputation for hospitality and western-type celebrations that was unmatched by any other town.

Vote, Vote, Vote—Time Is Flying Fast

> Rearing into action with a rip-snorting tail-tossing swapping of ends, and careening through three riotous days in a series of sun-fishing stiff-legged and blood-curdling bucks, the 1933 Stampede broke all records, from the first event on children's day to the breathless finish of the unbelievable mountain race.

Wow. The story in the *Williams Lake Tribune* for June 1933 certainly made that year's Stampede sound tremendously exciting. It had come a long way from its beginnings in July 1919, when people gathered near the Borland/Pinchbeck House (on the present Stampede grounds) for a day of cowboy sports to celebrate the coming of the Pacific Great Eastern Railway and the "birth" of the new village of Williams Lake. I'm sure no one then could have imagined a time when our little Stampede would be famous throughout Canada and the U.S.

The year 1933 was also memorable because it marked the first time a Williams Lake Stampede Queen was chosen—and by today's standards, the rules of the contest seem almost unbelievable.

> Some lucky maiden in this country-wide contest is going to preside over the three-day festivities. Ballot boxes will be in all stores and country places, and votes will be on sale at one nickel for twenty.

Yep, the contestant who sold the greatest number of tickets won the title and the crown. A giant thermometer was erected on contest chairman A.J. Tyson's drugstore, and the "mercury" rose

Rita Hamilton, 1935 Stampede Queen, leads the parade down Oliver Street. (COURTESY BUTCH RIFE)

steadily as each vote was recorded. The *Tribune* kept the delirium at fever pitch with this little ditty:

> Vote, vote, vote—make sure your Queen will win.
> Vote, vote, vote—the time is flying fast.
> Work till the last bally blinking vote is cast.

With six young women entered, a lively competition developed between two friends—Bernice Prior of Likely and Kathleen Spencer of Williams Lake. First Bernice was ahead, then Kathleen, with the latter taking a commanding lead in the last week. While this was going on, Kathleen's mother, Tissie, who was sure her daughter was going to win, handcrafted the all-important queen's crown out of cardboard with the help of her friend Edythe Hodgson. Painted silver and encrusted with simulated rhinestones and pearls, this delightful bit of memorabilia can be seen today at the Museum of the Cariboo-Chilcotin.

Then the tide turned. According to the late Marge Gillis, Bernice suddenly received some unusual and unsuspected support when "a kindly old prospector from Likely, just in from the hills and mining pits with his pockets full of gold, bought Bernice's entire stock of tickets." She had won.

As the lucky maiden, Bernice also won the big prize of "$25 cash and a ball-gown of her choice to the value of another twenty-five simoleons." Unable to find a suitable dress in the dusty little cowtown (population around 500), she borrowed a lovely satin wedding gown from good friend Georgina (Copley) Moon.

At the crowning ceremony in the old Stampede Hall on First Avenue, little Roy Crosina proudly carried in the crown on its velvet cushion, and it was placed on Bernice's head by pioneer Roderick Mackenzie.

The selling of votes went on until 1939, when both the Stampede and the contest were suspended during the war years. The Stampede was revived in 1947 and the queen contest in 1950, but this time with a big difference. There would now be a white queen and princess *and* a native queen and princess.

The same old system

Bernice Prior, centre, sold the most votes to become the first Stampede Queen in 1933. She is flanked by princesses Kathleen Spencer, left, and Vi Moon.

was in place, though; the girl who sold the most votes won, and that's what finally caused a great row in 1951. The girls found it embarrassing to go around selling tickets on themselves. "We feel like we are being raffled off," they said.

So the contest was dropped again and not revived until 1957, when for the first time the contestants were judged on "beauty, poise, personality, voice, dress and horsemanship"; there would be no buying of votes. White and native girls still competed separately, and the winners were announced at the Trail Riders' Playday in May.

Things continued this way until 1964, when new contest chairman Hilary Place made drastic changes, declaring there would now be only one queen and princess and they could be either white or Indian. "I felt it was racist," he declared later. "It shouldn't matter if the contestants are white, yellow, black, red, or green."

Two years later, Joan Palmentier of Riske Creek was the first native girl to be crowned Stampede Queen under the new rules.

By this time the role of Stampede royalty was changing. No longer did the queen just preside at Stampede events; she was attending functions at other centres throughout the year and competing at the national level. Joan Palmentier went on to be chosen B.C. Indian Princess, then Indian Princess of Canada in 1967; the prestigious Miss Rodeo Canada crown was won by Merry Ann Reed, Stampede Queen of 1975, and by Kelly Fredell in 1985.

Today the queen and her princesses are considered ambassadors—attractive and capable young women who can speak well and promote not only the Stampede but also the city wherever they go.

In 1933 the *Tribune* writer burbled with Stampede enthusiasm: "Gala streets, gorgeous weather, good-natured crowds, packed dance halls, colorful cowboys and cowgirls, beauty queens, jingle of spurs and creak of leather, all woven into a glamorous panorama of real Cariboo life."

And here we are in a new century and that decades-old description still fits.

Joan Palmentier, 1966 Stampede Queen, went on to become B.C Indian Princess, then Indian Princess of Canada in 1967. (WATERHOUSE PHOTO STUDIO)

The Wineglass

"We're still here over 100 years later," says Brian Durrell with understandable pride as he looks out over the lush benchlands beside the blue-green waters of the Chilcotin River that are part of the historic Wineglass Ranch established by his grandfather, Henry "Harry" Durrell.

The sixteen-kilometre trip from Highway 20 is not for the faint-hearted, and I couldn't help but be amazed at the courage and determination of the Durrell family in developing a ranch in such an inaccessible spot as I wound carefully down the single narrow track on a brilliant Sunday morning. Pot-holed and deeply rutted in spots, it switchbacked constantly around raw cliffs and teetered on the edge of deep gullies until it finally deposited me, thankfully, a thousand metres down among the fruit trees in this little bit of Eden.

"It was only accessible by horseback at first," says Brian. "Even later, when bringing in a piece of machinery, we would have to drag a log behind to act as a brake—and once down, it stayed here."

A road was started in 1946 but not completed until 1953. "We brought in the first tractor in 1959, but were still using horses for haying and putting up crops until 1964."

The story of the Durrell family begins, however, in Pembroke, Ontario, where Brian's grandfather, Henry Durrell, was born in 1870. He was just a young lad when he struck out on his own and headed west. Details are sketchy, but Brian believes his grandfather worked his way across the country and possibly even tried his luck at

First generation: Kate and Harry Durrell who established the Wineglass Ranch over 100 years ago.

Barkerville before finding work with Fred Beaumont on his River Ranch near Riske Creek.

There he obviously fell in love with the stark beauty of the Chilcotin River valley and first settled on a plateau west of Farwell Canyon.

"He started from scratch," says Brian, describing how his pioneer grandfather worked hard and acquired more and more land over the years, buying out or trading with neighbours until he owned property on both sides of the river

The year before his marriage in 1917 to Kathleen "Kate" McPhail, Harry built a permanent home and ranch buildings on the plateau north of Farwell Canyon. The couple had three children: Don, who was killed in World War II, Jack, and June (Klassen).

A quiet man, well read and respected, Harry was also very considerate and fair. During the flu epidemic of 1918, he often rode five miles over to the Toosey Reserve to chop wood and get water for the native people who were hit hard by the disease.

And let's not forget Kate, who endured the hardships and loneliness of life in the sparsely settled Chilcotin. "It's a great country for men, but hell on women," Harry was wont to say.

Sometime in the early 1940s, son Jack took over the management of the ranch for his aging parents. When Harry died in 1950 and Kate just a year later, their deaths almost ruined the ranch. "The death taxes were $80,000," explained Brian, and that, combined with low cattle prices, almost forced the family to sell.

*Second generation: Jack and Florence Durrell in their first tiny cabin
down by the Chilcotin River.*

But they hung on.

In the meantime, water had run out at the main ranch on the
plateau, and when Jack married Florence Cassils in 1949, the couple
decided to try their luck down beside the beautiful Chilcotin River
despite the difficulties of getting in and out.

They lived at first in a tiny cabin, then built a lovely log home
at what is now called the Home Ranch. Here they brought up their
three children: Don, Brian, and Linda.

"Everybody knew my dad," says Brian. "He was a people person,
keenly interested in everyone and everything." Jack was involved
in range management, very knowledgeable about native plants, and
fascinated by the history of the Chilcotin. A vintage car buff, he
was particularly proud of his beautifully restored Lincoln roadster,
which is still lovingly kept under wraps at the ranch.

Jack died in 1986, and since then the third generation of Durrells
has carried on. Don, who lives in Williams Lake, is engaged in logging,
but slim, quiet-spoken Brian is happy to manage the Wineglass with
the help of his family.

His sister, Linda, an avid birdwatcher, does the ranch books
and helps with farm work while wife Jane likes to ride, do "cow
work" as she calls it, and home-teach their three young children—
Erin, Keely, and Ian. Jane is of pioneer Cariboo stock too, and can
trace her roots back to the Eagles and Boitanos.

Brian's mother Florence still lives at the Home Ranch and cultivates a tremendous vegetable garden, enough for everyone.

Today the ranch is solidly efficient and supports a cow herd of 350 head. The original 160 acres has grown into an operation of more than 15,000 acres, which stretches for five miles along the Chilcotin River and ten miles up to the highway.

The Home Ranch complex sits in its own warm spot at 1,500 feet, surrounded by beautiful trees planted many years ago. "It has a little micro-climate of its own," smiles Jane. Apricots, grapes, cherries, plums, watermelons, walnuts, and transparent apples all grow in this green paradise.

In 1992 Brian and Jane moved the old log home in which Harry and Kate had started their married life up on the plateau 75 years earlier. The massive hand-hewn logs were transported down into the valley, where it was rebuilt as a guest house with a new roof, doors, windows, and even a modern bathroom.

Third generation: Jane Eagle and Brian Durrell on the deck of their modern home. (IRENE STANGOE PHOTO)

Incidentally, no one knows for sure, but it is believed the Wineglass gets its name from the cattle brand that Harry developed many years ago. It looks like, yes, a wine glass.

All uncredited photos courtesy of Brian Durrell.

Kate and Harry's original home after it was moved down into the valley and restored.

Durrell Butte

A high rocky ridge on the historic Wineglass Ranch was named Durrell Butte in 1994 by the province of B.C. to honour Sergeant Donald Durrell, who died in Germany while serving with the Royal Canadian Air Force during World War II.

The most westerly butte of Bald Mountain, it rises to a height of 5,000 feet and is especially prominent when observed from Highway 20 at the top of Lee's Hill. It was previously unnamed.

Born in 1921, Donald lived and worked all his short life at the Wineglass. He was just twenty years old when he enlisted with the RCAF and eventually became an air gunner. He was killed October 22, 1943, on a flight over Kassel, Germany, with his 49th RAF Squadron, and is buried in the Hanover British Cemetery in Germany.

The Tail End

This is not really history, just a "look back" at a dog who carved a little niche for himself in the memories of many Williams Lake residents who were here in the late 1950s and early 60s.

His name was Homer Stangoe and for a time he was the only basset hound in Williams Lake—a sloppy, ponderous beast with huge floppy ears who endeared himself to everyone and was welcome everywhere. Well, almost everywhere.

For years he ambled his sad, sorrowful way into homes, stores, schools, beer parlours, and even churches; traffic stopped so he could cross the street, and he regularly hitchhiked rides home. No social event was complete without his doleful appearance, and *Tribune* customers regularly had to step over his ungainly form as he lay sprawled on the front step or in the office.

Perhaps the most hilarious episode in Homer's chequered career was the time he followed his family to the United Church. At that time services were held in MacKinnon Hall until the church proper could be built. The stage was effectively hidden by red velvet curtains, and the altar with its candles, flowers, and an open Bible was exactly level with the stage. It was a setting for disaster.

I was playing for the services that fateful morning, when my young daughter Elaine appeared beside me, urgently whispering, "Mom, Homer's on the altar!"

I turned with disbelieving eyes to see Homer, his tremendous front paws firmly planted on the altar, staring mournfully with blood-shot eyes at the snickering congregation.

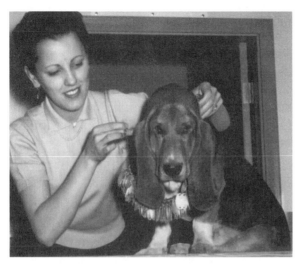

Town clerk Noreen Carson drapes Homer with a necklace of dog tags to publicize the deadline for 1961 dog licences. (COURTESY *WILLIAMS LAKE TRIBUNE*)

I was immobilized with horror, but my good friend Cathie Kerley quietly stepped into the breach and managed to coax Homer back through the velvet curtains, off the stage, then out an open basement door, all the time hoping he wouldn't give voice to deep baying howls of disapproval.

I managed to get my trembling fingers on the keys and was quietly awaiting the minister's arrival when Elaine appeared once more. "Don't look now, Mom, but Homer's on the altar again." Indeed he was. Finding another basement door open, he had plodded back upstairs and shuffled onto the altar to sniff the flowers, knocking the candles over in the process. By this time the congregation was in stitches.

Somehow I managed to pry myself off the piano bench and with Elaine's help coaxed our reluctant dog off the stage. As we pushed him down the steps, there was Todd Lee, our minister, coming up. "What will we do?" I wailed. He smiled gently and said "Perhaps he would like to take the service for me." We got Homer out the second open basement door, and finally the service got underway.

Then there was the hopeful chap who wanted him for breeding purposes. "Where's Homer going?" asked all the neighbourhood kids as our reluctant hound was pushed into the car. Caught off-guard, Clive replied, "Oh, cougar hunting." The idea of our pudgy, lethargic hound chasing cougars could make most people slightly hysterical, but the kids were suitably impressed and talked of Homer's hunting prowess for a long time. No little basset hounds ever appeared, however. You see, Homer was *very* reluctant.

Even his illnesses were unusual. I'd never known a dog to have tonsillitis until Homer came down with it—not once but three times—in 1963. At first, veterinarian Dr. John Roberts managed to control it with shots of penicillin and a huge bandage around his chest to stop him scratching, but the third time it erupted under his jaws and set him scratching from morning until night. This meant another trip to Dr. Roberts, who suggested I make booties for Homer's back paws.

"Booties?" I squawked. Fortunately for my sanity, Tony's Leather Shop was able to make leather booties. Despite his solid ungainly bulk, Homer periodically managed to get rid of them and, with maddening stupidity, would scratch himself raw again. Then Dr. Roberts fashioned a padded Elizabethan collar of tin that fitted around Homer's neck. Now a basset hound is a dolorously funny dog when he is absolutely normal; add an Elizabethan collar and you have a riot.

During his illness, Homer had to be kept in the house so he wouldn't wander away. (We couldn't tie him up as usual, because of his Elizabethan collar.) His constant despairing woofing at night in the basement was driving us almost wacky, so Clive developed a jacket out of an old army duffel bag with a handle on top so he could be tied up outside. This time Homer bore a striking resemblance to a suitcase. But he eventually recovered, and so did we.

Homer's biggest claim to fame, however, had to be his stage appearance.

Home economics teacher Belle Grattan had already produced two highly successful musical fashion shows when in 1961 she decided her third would be *The Boy Friend*, a fast-moving, funny musical of the 1920s.

I'll never forget my astonishment the morning Belle phoned to say: "I need a French poodle for my show, Irene, and I wondered if we could have Homer?"

Homer? "But Homer's a basset hound," I spluttered. She pointed out there were no poodles in town, and she figured our sloppy old beast would fit the bill nicely. And so help me, when the big night came, there it was on the program: "French poodle played by Homer Stangoe."

Despite misgivings from his family as to whether he might, er, misbehave, Homer, with perfect aplomb, waddled out onto the stage with Mlle. Dubonnet (Cheryl Stanchfield), surveyed the audience with sorrowful mien, and although it was not written in the script, disappeared into the tent with Mademoiselle while she was changing into her bathing costume. He brought down the house.

At the end, when the whole cast erupted onto the stage in a wild Charleston number, there was Homer in the middle, peering out with a bored nonchalant expression. Ah, what has Clark Gable got that I haven't got? he seemed to be saying.

Homer loved his family dearly, and after we became accustomed to his face, we loved him dearly too. He died of cancer in 1965.

The Road Runs North

The year 1958 was B.C.'s Centennial, marking 100 years since the Colony of British Columbia was formed. Clive and I had owned the *Tribune* for only eight years, but the publisher was determined to put out a special historical edition to mark the great occasion.

The news staff consisted of just the two of us, but undaunted we packed the two kids into the back of the station wagon whenever we had time that summer and wandered off into the wilds of the Cariboo-Chilcotin looking for stories.

Although we were a mite late and didn't get it out until January 1959, that special issue sold out and is a collector's item even today. I think Clive's most brilliant idea was to prevail upon our good friends noted playwright Gwen Pharis Ringwood and artist Sonia Cornwall respectively to write a narrative poem for the front cover and to illustrate it. Entitled simply "The Road," it was truly beautiful.

Gwen Ringwood

When surgeon Dr. Barney Ringwood decided to join his friend Dr. Hugh Atwood in practice at Williams Lake in 1953, the town got an added bonus. Along with Dr. Ringwood came his wife, gifted author and playwright Gwen Pharis Ringwood. Considered one of the founders of theatre arts in Western Canada, she had already created an impressive number of plays and stories by the time she moved to the Cariboo.

She soon became the driving force behind the revitalized Williams Lake Players Club, writing and directing many plays as well as producing humorous skits for coffee houses and other social events.

She is probably best remembered locally for the magnificent musical *The Road Runs North*, which she wrote and directed in collaboration with musician Art Rosoman to celebrate Canada's 1967 Centennial. With a cast of 60, the rollicking yet touching gold-rush tribute to B.C.'s past played to packed houses every night.

In appreciation of her work, an amphitheatre in Boitanio Park was named the "Gwen Pharis Ringwood Theatre" when it officially opened in 1971. Unfortunately, due to vandalism and deterioration, it had to be torn down in 1985.

Over the years, Gwen received many awards, including the Eric Hamber Trophy, B.C.'s most prestigious theatre honour; and two doctorates—one from the University of Victoria, the other from the University of Lethbridge; and was the subject of two books—one an anthology of her plays, the other on her life and creative ability. She had become a legend in her own time.

Gifted author and playwright Gwen Pharis Ringwood.

Gwen was still writing and painting up until her death in May 1984 at her home at Chimney Lake. Many of her plays are considered classics and are still being performed today by theatre groups throughout the continent.

Sonia Cornwall

Sonia Cornwall has lived in the 150 Mile area most of her life, and her paintings are a strong reflection of her love of the Cariboo-Chilcotin.

Although she has had no formal art training, her work is well known across Canada. She has had one-person shows in Vancouver, Victoria, Kamloops, and Prince George as well as Williams Lake and many other interior towns.

Sonia inherited her talent from her mother, Vivien Cowan, who was also a noted artist and founding president of the Cariboo Art Society. As a child growing up at their home on the Onward Ranch south of Williams Lake, Sonia was given paints to play with on rainy days, but she didn't get serious about art until much later in life. After finishing her education at the Strathcona school at Shawnigan Lake, she came back to Williams Lake to work on the ranch, driving tractor, ploughing fields, and helping with roundups, especially during

Talented Cariboo artist Sonia Cornwall. (COURTESY *WILLIAMS LAKE TRIBUNE*)

the war years. Married in 1947 to Hugh Cornwall, grandson of pioneer Clement Cornwall of Ashcroft, the couple later moved to Jones Lake Ranch. It wasn't until her two daughters had started school that she returned to her early love and began painting in earnest—and has never looked back.

Although Sonia's work was greatly influenced by famed Group of Seven painter A.Y. Jackson, who was a frequent visitor to the Onward in the 1950s and 60s, she has developed her own distinctive impressionist style. Holiday trips to Mexico and Fiji have resulted in some brilliant canvasses of those exotic countries, but mostly her paintings depict the magnificent Cariboo ranching country that she knows so well.

THE ROAD
A narrative poem written by the late Gwen Pharis Ringwood
(reprinted with permission from her family)

The road runs North, East and North at the beginning.
I've followed it many times,
Away from the city of glass and lights and flowers.
Away from the sea and the delta and the flowers
Into the shining mountains, wreathed with mist.

(This mystery of mist and mountain gives rise to legend.
Men say—those who return have said—that giant footprints
Track the white-walled caverns at the ridge;
And when the moon's round in October, strange fires
Come from a crag where no fire should be.
I cannot vouch for this having ventured no trail
Away from the beaten path.)

At Hope I'd place a warning. "Traveller, Beware!
Look not too long upon the mountains here
Lest you be drawn to their snow-cowled serenity
To search for Shangri-la, and find oblivion."

Even in August the heart grows cold remembering that December
When the plane mounted the prairie skies over the jewelled city,
Flashed holiday farewell, and then flew westward
Into the shrouded dark.
Somewhere in the high, impersonal majesty of these peaks
The plane and all its passengers went down.
Keeping, as all must keep, the unknown, unscheduled appointment,
The traveller on the road remembers them.

The road runs North into the cedared canyon.
Rain-heavy fern lean toward the gorge
And rock, slow-dying, battles the ancient river.

Salmon run here
Dig the years down to the stone-tipped arrow or beyond,
Still the indomitable one, noses up stream
Making the unbelievable journey from the sea
Back to the cell-known sand to spawn and die.

Now the road skirts the canyon roof, edges the cliff
Where Indian traffickers carrying canoes
Clung to sheered rock, swung out on thonged ladders,
And smiled at the white-faced Englishmen who followed.
"The very rocks are worn with footprints
Where it seems no man could travel," Fraser wrote,
Then following his guides, he and his men inched toward the ocean,
Looking up and ahead, not down.

And the young engineers! They built the first road here.
Did they sing as they hacked at granite?
Send their shouts echoing against the far canyon wall
Or curse at the rock and the sullen river and the cold?
Perhaps on some tree nearby a boy from Surrey carved his name
A tree can span a century, outlast a man.
The tree could stand.

Past Hell's Gate now, past the long finger of sand
Where ten thousand miners built their fires,
Ate, drank, brawled, bent to the sluice box,
Weighted in the day's bright harvest, and at night
Dreamed of the mother lode.

(There in the falling dark a small Chinese
Pig-tailed and alien dug at the gravel
Gabbled of home and family
"Oh Honourable Son, remember me—
I have found jade here, not so good as ours
But carved it could pass for ours.
I send it to you. And gold, I will find gold and send it
That you may bury me beside my ancestors,
My Son remember me."
But the small Chinese body lies, at the last, pine-boxed
In a shallow grave beside the river, no longer alien.)

The man-loved Thompson, blue as heaven
Loses itself in the old angry Fraser,
And the trail splits, one arm to Lillooet.
The road runs North,
Runs through the desert, knotted with sage and cactus,
Ringed with blue hills where hooded rock
Harbors the rattlers. Coil on coil,
Cold comfort to each other, they wait blind for spring.

Above us, they tell me, are marks of the old road.
Could that be it? Grooved by the wheels of stagecoach
and the feet of eight bay horses carrying the mail?
Was it here the desperadoes cached the gold?
Did the cracked hooves of camels stir this dust?
Camels! Stable them elsewhere. Get them away!
My horse and mules go crazy at their stink!
Keep your cud-chewing abortions of Arabia away!
So the patient pariahs of the East, bearing their packs
Humped North to winter, where they caught cold and died.

The roads runs North
Long beneedled pine give way to jackpine
And in September the burning poplars bend to the quiet lake.
Idly the drowsy cattle winnow swamp hay under the thin-leafed willow.

The soft stare of cattle holds some enveloping strangeness
Bland, benign, that eases the heart.
Fortunate too the traveller who for a single intake of the breath
Looks deep into the star eyes of a deer
For henceforth he knows that time can form crystals
Precise and luminous.

An old stopping house, rebuilt for tourist,
Houses the ghosts of dance-hall girls, laced and beribboned,
Of bearded miners and the wanderers following the trail,
Seeking each one his own adventure or his grail.
Some found the gold. Some died. Some went away.
A few stayed on to raise wheat or cattle
or run a flour mill beside a stream.
Leaving their children land beside good water,
Beside the blue Chilcotin or the Fraser or a fringed lake
Where ducks nest in the tall reeds in April.

The rest are gone now, gone with the old road and the gold
And the years.
Gone now, all, all long gone and yet
Sometimes at evening
when the wind stirs the pine boughs
When the sound of the gaunt, unyielding river
comes up from the canyon,
When wild geese, soft crying each to each
Thrust North in a thin, black arrow
Then they are here again, the travellers,
The motley, brawling, strange, adventurous travellers
Explorers and the Indians who taught them,
Trader for furs, prospector and miner,
Engineer, ship builder, teamster.
Storekeeper, cattleman, miller,
Adventurer, gambler, parson
The lusty, hungry, boisterous travellers
Touched with the bright brush of courage
Their names sound in the wind's sigh
And in the cry of birds,

And in the voice of the old river
And the traveller on the road remembers them.

The road runs North
I followed it first a stranger.
I follow it now remembering those who came this way before me.
I follow it now to a small pool of light
That circles, so briefly, all that I know as home.

Index

Looking Back
at the Cariboo-Chilcotin

Cariboo-Chilcotin
Pioneer People and Places

Irene Stangoe

ISBN 1-895811-25-2
5½ X 8½ • 160 pages
Softcover • $14.95

ISBN 1-895811-12-0
5½ X 8½ • 128 pages
Softcover • $12.95

Encouraged by the response to her first book, *Cariboo-Chilcotin: Pioneer People and Places*, which was selected for *B.C. Bookworld*'s all-time top 200 list, Irene created a second collection of heritage stories set in B.C.'s Interior. Blending fact, legend, and local hearsay, Irene entertains in a folksy, down-home voice. Drawn from historical files and the memories of those who were there, these stories are dotted with ghost towns and colourful pioneers. Irene Stangoe has been a newspaperwoman for over 45 years. Her "Looking Back" column in the *Williams Lake Tribune* has been going strong since 1975.